ROCK YOUR RENTAL

ROCK YOUR RENTAL

Style, Design, and Marketing Tips to Boost Your Bookings

Joanne and Rosanne Palmisano

The Countryman Press

A division of W. W. Norton & Company

Independent Publishers Since 1923

This book is for Mom and Dad.
Thanks for teaching us the joy of spontaneous travel,
from Sunday drives on a country road to weekend
trips to the beach. We remember it all.

For information about permission to reproduce selections from this book, write to
Permissions, The Countryman Press, 500 Fifth Avenue, New York, NY 10110

For information about special discounts for bulk purchases, please contact
W. W. Norton Special Sales at specialsales@wwnorton.com or 800-233-4830

Manufacturing by ToppanLeefung
Book design by Jesse Pakenham, Folk House Design
Production manager: Devon Zahn

The Countryman Press
www.countrymanpress.com

A division of W. W. Norton & Company, Inc.
500 Fifth Avenue, New York, NY 10110
www.wwnorton.com

978-1-68268-498-6 (pbk.)

10 9 8 7 6 5 4 3 2 1

Everyone loves before-and-afters, so we filled the book with them! Enjoy!

After

Contents

Introduction

Before we get started on sharing our professional business and design experiences with you, let us introduce ourselves. Yes, it's cool that we are identical twins. And we travel . . . a lot. But what is even cooler is what our experience as designers, project managers, marketers, and travelers has taught us about the competitive short-term vacation rental market. In this book, we've combined our talents to bring you unique and budget-friendly design and marketing ideas that can help you stand out as a property owner. These ideas are also relevant if you own or manage a boutique hospitality business, such as a bed-and-breakfast, inn, or motel.

Our design work and Joanne's design books have been featured in the *Wall Street Journal, Boston Globe, Chicago Tribune, Dwell, Washington Post, USA Today, Lonny, Apartment Therapy, Better Homes & Gardens, Country Living, Outside, Old House Journal, PopSugar, Flea Market Style, Cottage Country, House Crashers*, DIY Network, and HGTV . . . just to name a few.

Damn, look how cute we are! Besides being identical twins, things we have in common include our love for our mother's spaghetti sauce, exceptional work ethics, career success, and a passion for what we do. From a young age we worked hard, whether it was washing dishes, selling Christmas trees, sorting tomatoes, or picking up golf balls. Today, in our careers as successful entrepreneur and global executives, we still believe that a customer's positive experience is at the heart of any thriving business.

Joanne Palmisano

Joanne is an award-winning interior designer. She specializes in rental properties, inns, motels, boutique hotels, and restaurants that want a unique and personal look. She is the author of three internationally acclaimed design books, *Salvage Secrets*, *Salvage Secrets Design & Décor*, and *Styling with Salvage*, a contributing designer for DIY Network, and a stylist for hospitality and lifestyle brands and magazines. She owns and has owned numerous rental properties, from long term to short term.

Joanne started in hospitality after college as a tour leader traveling from inn to inn throughout New England. She then went into the marketing and customer service field for over 15 years, including an executive director role at the Make-A-Wish Foundation of Vermont, and the creator of the *Vermont Wedding Resource Guide*, working with numerous boutique hotels and inns, before her passion for design became her career.

Today, she combines her hospitality experience and rental ownership knowledge to create personality-filled designs that help increase demand and profits. For the past 10 years, Joanne has traveled across the country speaking about designing with recycled, salvaged, and vintage material and the importance of adding character to our homes and businesses.

Joanne is an avid traveler, and she especially loves to travel when her twin sister, Rosanne, plans the entire trip and she just goes along for the ride (but don't tell Rosanne that).

Rosanne Palmisano

Rosanne has been a brand and marketing strategist professional for over 20 years for global companies that everyone knows and loves, including Pearl Izumi, The North Face, Nike, The Gap, Icebreaker, and Pact Apparel. She has worn many hats throughout her career, from global events manager to international brand manager to CEO/CMO.

Today, she runs Little Giants Collaborative, a consulting firm that helps companies with brand, go-to-market, digital, and marketing strategies. She has a passion for home renovation and has been the general contractor for most of her own projects as well as renovating and designing several other homes. Her homes have appeared in national magazines, which has led many friends (and developers) to ask for her design help. Over the last few years, Rosanne has designed at least half a dozen vacation rental properties in Sonoma County, California.

Rosanne is a United Airlines million miler, and she has been fortunate enough to live and travel around the world for her career. Her lodging experiences have varied dramatically, from a middle-of-nowhere small farm hotel in India to a sheep's sheering shed (say that 10 times fast) in New Zealand to the extraordinary country residence Hotel Villa Cipriani in Asolo, Italy, to a tiny cabin in a 36-foot sailboat, and on and on and on. Rosanne has an excellent understanding of customers' expectations based on her personal and professional experience. She is a *big* believer in reading and writing reviews!

Why We Wrote This Book

Why did we write this book, you ask? Well, one night, in Capri, Italy, after one too many glasses of vino (that's one of the 10 Italian words we know), we thought, *How cool would it be if we combined our talents and many years of experience to offer candid, easy, affordable design and marketing advice to those who need it?* (And our experience tells us there's a lot of you.) We sketched out an outline on a paper placemat, and the next morning . . . we still thought it was a great idea!

We want to help hardworking folks who own inns, bed-and-breakfasts, boutique hotels, and vacation rental homes to stand out in the competitive market. We can't help ourselves. When we check into a new place, be it a hotel room or an apartment rented through Airbnb, VRBO, Booking.com, or a similar site, we find ourselves immediately going over all the details of the space: what we love, what could be improved, how the owners could market better to increase their bookings, and so on. (But then we worry—if they do all this, will we be able to afford to come back?)

Improving your property doesn't necessarily mean pricing your previous customers out of returning. It's a fine line, but at the end of the day, we can help. Making some small, significant changes can make a big difference and help you strike that balance. We want you all to succeed and be your best—and hopefully you'll remember us and give us the "friends and family" rate the next time!

Combined, we have over 25 years' experience in business, marketing, customer service, and design (actually more, but we don't want to feel old). Over the past few years, we've been hired to design, decorate, and market vacation rental properties, motels, and inns. Our collaboration is naturally complementary, in large part because we have different likes and needs when it comes to staying in a rental property. For instance, Joanne is all about the cozy clean blankets, whereas Rosanne is all about making sure she can get good Wi-Fi service. What we do have in common is that we know, no matter the cost or size of the place, vacation rental owners and boutique hospitality managers can create fabulous experiences for their guests and stand out from the crowd.

We put together this book, *Rock Your Rental,* and filled it with design, marketing, and customer service ideas to help you develop a unique personality for your rental. If you want to *rock* it out of the park and stay competitive in this ever-increasing (and in some places, saturated) rental market, then you have to be willing to go the extra mile. If you are passionate about your guests' experience and about adding value to their stay, then this process will feel less like work and more like the fun and exciting side of being a property owner.

This book covers the importance of your personal design and how it affects your guests' experience from start to finish, from the moment they see your listing to the second they leave your property and tell their friends about it. It is your go-to handbook for simple, affordable, actionable tips, and it contains stories, examples, and ideas that can help you increase your bookings, profits, and customer happiness.

Rock Your Rental does *not* include information about investing in real estate, cash flows, booking (hosting) platforms, vacation rental rules, regulations, laws, and all the other fun operational parts that you need to know to run a successful hospitality space. There are some amazing resources for that side of the business, including the excellent *Get Paid for Your Pad* by Jasper Ribbers and Huzefa Kapadia, and Richard Fertig's binge-worthy YouTube channel, STRU (Short Term Rental University). In Chapter 4 of this book we list a large number of resources to help you rock your rental. Don't get overwhelmed. Just take it one step at a time.

We sincerely hope this book helps you. You may love all our ideas, you may love half our ideas, at times you might even think, "Tell me something I don't already know." Great! That means you're already on the right track. But if even one of the ideas you find here changes the way you do business for the better—we're happy and your guests will be happier! We have found through our research (and sleeping around) that a surprising number of places do not even nail the basics. And, as we all know, it's the little things that matter.

Disclaimer

Okay, here is the part nobody loves . . . rules. This is also where we are going to state a disclaimer. In the design advice that follows, we obviously have no idea of either the specifications of the space you're working with or the circumstances of your location. For example, regulations, fire codes, structural codes, vacation rental laws, and home association rules differ by city and state (and country!), and it's incumbent on you as the property owner to understand them before you start tearing out walls! Every town, city, and state also has specific rules, codes, and laws regarding vacation rental properties—some are adding more every day.

So before you start sledge hammering that old bathroom tile or digging a hole in the backyard for that fire pit, check your state and local codes and building restrictions. You don't want a massive mess with permitting problems, code infractions, or HOA (homeowner association) issues. As we share our design ideas, all we ask is that you don't break the law, the bank, or worse, your spirit.

We are here to help. Have fun!

XOXO
Joanne and Rosanne

Chapter ①

Who Are Your Guests?
Why Are You Redesigning?

Design plays a key role in your marketing. Your first impulse might be to run out and get some throw pillows and start posting shots on Instagram. But let's brainstorm first. Before you delve into designing your rental, you should do a little homework. In this chapter, we show you how a thoughtful design helps you create unique spaces that will appeal to your target audience. We have some clever, straightforward, and budget-friendly design ideas, which in turn, should increase the number of stays in your space and improve the profitability of your business. But first you need to answer a few questions to establish a few things: Who is your target audience? What is your budget? And why is a redesign important to you? Your answers to these questions will help you determine what your design will look like in the end.

Joanne was the interior designer for this private vacation home renovation project in southern Vermont. This master bedroom shows just how simple and inviting your design and décor can be. Although this is a small room, it looks larger because the shot was taken from the doorway. This perspective allows as much of the room as possible to be in the shot while showing its relationship to the other rooms, including the bathroom with the salvaged barn wood sliding door.

This is a great example of Less Is More. There wasn't a lot of need for décor and styling in the space—just a modern bed frame, a stunning rug, a gorgeous blanket, and a modern lumbar pillow with colors that match the rest of the space. Each of these functional elements play a key role in the design and Joanne worked hard to keep the design simple, inviting, and filled with personality, while still keeping the character of the structure, which is what drew the family to the building in the first place. Remember, your guests want to feel like they are away from home, a place that feels different and inviting, and that creates an experience for them.

Facts and Stories

No matter how beautiful your place is, location is everything. Location, location, location . . . there is a reason people say it three times. Regardless of your personal circumstances—unless you are famous, have an amazing following online, or know of a town or neighborhood that is about to become the next hot spot—the location of your property will always play a key role in your bookings and who makes them. With that said, also keep in mind that if you have a really special, unique property, there are people who will seek it out no matter its location.

Know Thy Customer—Your Peeps

Maybe you're saying, "I already know who my peeps are, they're my current guests. Tell me something I don't know." But what if you want different guests? Or what if you're getting bad reviews, because your current guests aren't the right fit for your property? Perhaps you are getting lots of families, but they complain about the noise coming from a loud, happening bar nearby that stays open until 2 a.m. If so, then maybe your peeps should be young, hip couples. What if you're getting young, hip couples but you would rather host retired couples who enjoy having a glass of wine with you but are just as happy reading a book in a quiet space? Let's get to the root of it.

How you design and market your property will help you attract the guests you want and, by default, improve your online reviews. If you are posting photos of cute young ladies who look like Instagram influencers hanging out (an excellent example is Urban Cowboy, a boutique hotel and bed-and-breakfast), then you'll probably attract young, cool hipsters. If you're posting photos of babies, or show cribs in every room, then obviously you will attract families with young children. If you highlight one-level living, or retirement-friendly amenities, then you will attract guests who value those things.

We know you're open to everyone, but in reality you can't be all things to all people. If your space has a million stairs and bunk beds only, you probably will not market yourself to an elderly crowd. There is a different group (or two or three) that better aligns with your space and offerings. These people will make up the majority of your guests (or who you want to be the majority of your guests). So take a moment to look at who you are serving *now* and who you *want* to serve in the future. Take the time to think in-depth about who your ideal customers are.

Homework: Complete an Audience Profile form for each of your target markets. This particular worksheet is geared toward the travel information. You can change the questions to be more relevant to your particular situation.

RESEARCH: IDENTIFY YOUR AUDIENCE MOTIVATIONS & ENGAGEMENT

Identifying your primary, secondary and tertiary audiences will allow you to focus your marketing and content strategies . . . which will improve your qualified leads and conversion. You can't be everything to everyone . . . so find your peeps and understand why they want to book with you.

What are their needs in a vacation rental? Why would they want to stay with you over others? How do they learn about you? What are their demographics and psychographics?

PRIMARY: x

SECONDARY: x

TERTIARY: x

Create a Profile for Your Target Person

Age:
Occupation:
Family Life:

Income:
Location:
Avg Travel:

PICTURE
of Your Target
Person

Buying value:

My Travel Style:

My Travel Goals and Values:

My Travel Frustrations and Fears:

Where I get my information before I make travel decisions?:

My influencer channels?:   My social channels?:   My go-to research for travel?:

My favorite activities?:   My top MUST-HAVE in lodging?:   My do-not-like in lodging?:

JOANNE PALMISANO

Age: 50ish
Occupation: Interior Designer
Family Life: Married/Children

Income: Gazzillionaire (she wishes)
Location: Vermont, New England
Avg Travel: 10 x year

Buying value: Super conscious on what she spends her money on. Experiences are more important than material goods.

My travel style: Varies drastically. "When I travel with my friends or sisters it's to explore . . . mainly to hike and eat. On these trips I prefer to spend less $ on lodging to extend the vacation days. When I travel with my family it's important to me they have a great time and I will spend more on accommodations and amenities to make sure everyone in the family enjoys their vacation. When I'm traveling alone for work it depends on the location . . . if it's a cool city I want to explor look for a vacation rental for a unique place to stay and visit as well as feel safe. If it's not a cool location, I look for the closet, safest and cleanest hotel next to the conference.

My travel goals and values:
- I like finding locations where I can combine outdoor activities (hiking) with culture. Like Italy.
- I like finding unique places that are in my budget . . . it's a like a treasure hunt for me.
- It's important to me there is sustainability efforts happening at places I stay and visit.

My travel frustrations and fears:
- If I am traveling alone, safety is always at the top of my mind. Unlit entrances and dark parking lots drive me crazy.
- Dirty Bathrooms. Enough said. Wait . . . moldy, smelly places. Old sheets or bedding. Really?
- When I arrive and it doesn't look like the pictures at all. I was over promised . . . now I'm pissed.

Where I get my information before I make travel decisions:
- Internet—I do a lot of research. I'm a visual person so pictures are important and if something catches my eye, I'll start reading the reviews.
- While traveling, if I come across a place I want to visit or stay on my next trip, I grab a card.
- I have champagne taste on a beer budget. So I subscribe to numerous e-newsletter and search Pinterest where I look for "specials, deals" and so on during the off-season.

My influencer channels:
- *Travel & Leisure* eNews
- *Budget Travel* Magazine
- VRBO newsletter
- Instagram Influencers

My social channels:
- Instagram
- Pinterest
- Facebook
- YouTube & podcasts

My go-to research for travel:
- Google Flights
Visual first so design matters during my initial search
- Google—Lodging
- Booking.com
- Tablet.com

My favorite activities:
- Hiking
- Eating—cute cafes
- Finding salvage yards
- Markets
- Reading on beach
- Exploring Italy

My top must-haves in lodging:
- Comfortable bed and pillows
- Place to sit and read
- Natural light
- Seems obvious—CLEAN
- Good WI-FI
- Friendly staff/interaction

My top do-not-like in lodging:
- Hard pillows (and only 1)
- Dark rooms
- Uncomfortable toilets
- Dirty (any part)
- Unfriendly staff
- Unclear check-in/directions

Before

DESIGN THOUGHT PROCESS: REARRANGING THE BATHROOM

For this small, private vacation home in the woods, Joanne used the old wood from the exterior to create a sliding door (which helps save space). The floor is local Vermont slate and the vintage brown dresser was given a dark black stain. With subway tile, light grout, a round mirror, and modern lighting, the bathroom now has a contemporary farmhouse feel. The two unique character pieces, the barn door and the vintage dresser (about $100), really give the design a wow feel and complement the modern pieces well.

Everything is not only up to code, but it is so energy efficient that it won an award. When you're upgrading a space like this, don't be afraid to move things around—especially if the plumbing is easily accessible in the basement or crawlspace and you're just moving one plumbing fixture to another location. In this bathroom, moderately priced materials were used. What significantly added to the costs had to do with time and effort—the labor, construction, and amount of renovation and retrofitting that needed to be done. Yes, moving plumbing fixtures *will* cost you more, but as you crunch the numbers consider whether the change will bring more comfort to your guests. In the hospitality game, comfort is king!

After

One of our biggest challenges is explaining to owners and managers how important it is to really know their target customers before beginning to design or market a property. Rosanne will not start a project without knowing a client's end goals or the intended customer that a given product/service is meant to help and why. (She is a bit annoying that way.) Some may call her Little General (yes, a family nickname), but her success has proven the importance of starting with the end in mind. Joanne is more easily distracted by shiny objects. Thankfully, she lets Rosanne do most of the marketing.

The following questions come from a target market worksheet that Rosanne takes clients through as they begin this discovery phase of "*Who* is my customer?" Key questions to ask yourself are:

- **What** do I have to offer my customer that is special, different, and relevant?
- **Where** do I communicate or interact with them (online, emails, e-newsletter, mailing, print magazines)?
- **Why** am I important in their lives?

Even if you get to only your primary target audience, you are that much closer to connecting with your guests.

Fill out the Identify Target Market form and the Audience Profile form (see pages 21 and 22) and refer to them often as you consider your design and décor. Does what you're doing reflect your target guests' needs and wants? If not, go back to the design concept drawing board.

Know Thyself—What Makes You So Special?

Why is it important to know how special you are? It's because knowing who you are will help you stand out in a crowded market! Figuring out your brand and design style will help you align with the guests you would like to attract. It is crucial to do this before you do any design work or marketing. This will help you focus because you can't be everything to everyone. Know who you are . . . and who you are not. Your design should reflect this.

If your design reflects who you are, your customers will appreciate your authenticity. We have worked with inns, motels, and other vacation rental property owners who have done amazing jobs on their renovations, increasing their booking rates by eight times more than they predicted. And even

Joanne with Eliza, the owner of Main + Mountain Bar & Motel in Ludlow, Vermont (formerly the All Seasons Motel that Eliza and her partner, Justin, bought at a real estate auction), on photo shoot day. Joanne created the concept design for the renovation of the motel and Rosanne was charged with the marketing—including branding and strategy. Wonder Twins powers in action.

Joanne has about three drinks a month, but for some crazy reason she always seems to be caught with a drink in her hand when a camera is around. At Lawson's Finest Liquids Taproom in Waitsfield, Vermont, where she was the interior designer for the project, she is enjoying the fruits of her labor. Joanne designed this space to reflect Lawson's target audiences . . . beer lovers, as well as folks who love authentic, unique, and approachable gathering spaces.

after all that, they have hosted that one guest who didn't like what they did. The guest didn't like the changes, the décor, or even the feel of sun on their face. . . . Yes, there are times a customer will have a legitimate complaint, but be aware that there are people you will never be able to please. With that caveat in mind, your goal is to establish and build on what makes you so special to 99 percent of the folks who will be staying with you.

A good way to help you figure out what makes you special is to put your look and feel on paper before you do anything else. Throughout this book we'll have you research some design ideas, do some homework, create your brand identity, and more. How's that for first-rate fun!

Know Thy Design Budget

Let's talk about design and décor budgets. These budgets are distinct from other business concerns, be it operational budgets or buying buildings or making loan payments. What we are talking about here is money for small design changes and/or moderate renovations to create unique spaces that don't cost a fortune.

We are going to oversimplify here and talk about three main types of vacation rental categories that, in turn, may affect your budget decisions. Obviously, your situation may be more complex, but you can use this as a guideline for determining your needs.

Category 1

Your property is 100 percent investment, and it is run as a business. In this case, you're crunching your numbers for the best return on investment (ROI). This space is designed just for your guests—this will not be a personal design project. It's surprising how frequently we need to remind our clients that they will not be living in this property, so items like a $3,000 glass and gold-leaf coffee table is probably not the wisest purchase. Run your numbers to see how much of your profit you can spend on design, which in turn will help you get more bookings and so increase the profitability of your rental.

Category 2

If your property is a rental as well as your personal vacation home (part profit, part fun), then you may be more willing to spend money on some-

Homework: Ask yourself a few questions to make sure you understand your property and your budget:

- What is your property to you? Investment only or personal enjoyment as well?

- Which category do you fit in?

- How will you budget the design improvements for your property?

thing that is meaningful to your enjoyment (that Viking range that brings out the inner chef in you, or the deck furniture that you've coveted for years). If you live there even part time, you need and deserve to enjoy it as much as your guests. So we're okay with you allocating your budget differently than you might for Category 1.

Category 3

This is your future retirement home. Although you don't live there now, you will later on. In the meantime you want it to earn a profit or cover its costs. Or you just want to have people in there enjoying it. You know that you will likely renovate, furnish, or do something differently with it when you finally arrive for that chapter in your life. So for now, you may want to renovate in a way that handles the long-term changes that you don't want to do twice—for example, installing classic tile or hardwood floors. As for the furnishings and décor, you should consider how your design fits the style, taste, and needs of your guests.

Why is identifying your category important? Because how you design, how much you spend, and what you choose as priorities will be different depending on what the property means to you. You may personally love the mid-century look, but if your vacation rental is in wine country, then farmhouse modern will rent out much more frequently and at a higher rate, because that is the demand for such a location. Depending on your situation, you will need to consider forgoing your favorite style for one that works with the property and competition. Lucky for you, we have found ourselves in these exact situations, and so we have some experience with saving clients from making design mistakes. Are you seeing where we are going with this? Okay, your turn . . . homework!

After

Before

DESIGN THOUGHT PROCESS: SIMPLE CHANGES . . . BIG RESULTS

When Joanne was hired to create a fun and inviting vacation rental design for a family who purchased a lake home in southern Vermont, she understood their goal was to retire there in about 15 years. Their budget was not large and they weren't ready to do a full renovation, but they wanted it to be comfortable enough for guests and for when they came to enjoy the lake house themselves.

Joanne started by painting the walls a soothing and warm, soft color. Then she added simple (but sturdy) black metal platform bed frames, great mattresses, comfortable bedding, and white linens. She introduced a pop of color with the cotton throw blankets, and the homeowner painted an old dresser the same bright blue. Joanne purchased a royalty-free photo from Shutterstock and had it blown up to the size of the headboard wall (on sticky back paper) at her local printing shop for a couple hundred dollars. Two plug-in wall sconces (we didn't want to add hardwiring to the budget) were easily placed on the wall above the beds. Then for the listing photo shoot, we added a vintage vase and some ferns we picked outside. Done! A simple, affordable, but dramatic transformation that has proved hugely popular with guests and the homeowner alike, all for less than a thousand dollars in total.

Research Design Ideas

What type of project are you doing? One room? A whole apartment? An entire motel? What items are priorities? What are your guests saying about your space currently? Online reviews are a great place to start to do your research and see what folks love and don't love. Read between the lines: "tired" and "outdated" are the sort of phrases that mean a property is due for an overhaul.

Keep asking questions. What are the issues and concerns with the existing space? Are they outdated? Do they feel cluttered? Are the rooms dark? Too little furniture? Too much furniture? Does the flow work? Does it stand out in a crowd? You may have a feeling for this, but we hope once you've done some design research and have read through this book, you'll be more open to making changes that you may have not otherwise considered.

Before

Within the image, partial text is visible:

I rolling hillsides and
...ain backdrops stir the soul
...ake each day simply
...sible to compare...

...ton Range, at the heart of
...traordinary place, stands
...7,000 ft above Jackson Hole.
...f the Rockies, the Grand,
...e and South Tetons are at the
... of the range with an apex
...70 feet. They were formed
...n years ago and continue
...e Tetons are the
...untains in the world.

After

DESIGN THOUGHT PROCESS: CREATING LOCAL EXPERIENCES

This before-and-after is a downtown motel redo, Mountain Modern Motel, in Jackson Hole, Wyoming, done by the amazingly talented firm TruexCullins Architecture and Interior Design, for which Joanne was part of the design team. Over a hundred motel rooms were transformed from outdated and rundown to international award-winning.

   The motel is a big hit with the guests, town, and community. The design is modern and unique, while the style fits the adventurer, traveler, and businessperson alike. This was a large project (with investors), and the goal was to modernize the space as well as give it a distinct personality and sense of place (while keeping within the budget). If you look at the before photo and didn't know where it was located, would you guess it to be in the awesome town of Jackson Hole? Never!

Spend some time looking at locations that are similar to yours and see what catches your eye. The gallery wall, the bright outdoor beach chairs, the simple bedding . . . what are the common denominators that make people stop scrolling through hundreds if not thousands of options and spend a little more time actually reading the listing? What type of properties are the most sought after in your area? Do you want to stand out from that or blend in? We hope a little of both!

Throughout this book, we showcase a few tried-and-true ideas that can give your rooms the wow factor that guests are looking for. Obviously, there are innumerable ways to add the wow, but we hope these will get your own creative juices flowing.

As part of the new interactive design for Mountain Modern Motel, we added a nice local feature: a description of the Teton Range next to the wall mural mountain photo. Other new features included a small word search over the table for guests to play with. There are also topographical maps in the bathroom, with a sliding mirror that reveals the entire local map so that guests can get a feel for the area and know exactly where they are—that is, a cool motel in a hip, adventurous Western town! We also reused the headboards, covered them in faux leather, and added a variety of carpet tiles in bright colors to make the carpeting a bold statement. (We used eco-friendly tiles by Interface.) Notice the datum line running through the room that divides the darker paint on the bottom of the wall and white on the top. A design touch like this is an easy way to add character to a space. These are just a few of the features that dramatically changed the rooms of Mountain Modern Motel and gave them a sense of place, personality, and a warm, inviting feel.

Design Homework

In order to get to know your authentic design style and styles that would work for your customers, start your own Pinterest page for your place (keep it a secret page), and then look at the pages of other creative folks. Have tabs on your page for bathrooms, bedrooms, public spaces, marketing ideas, etc., and then start pinning images of looks you like and design ideas that would work with your space. This Pinterest page will be different than your Pinterest account that you will set up for marketing your rental—more on that later.

To get started, you can check out the pages of some creative folks and places we love. Of course, we could have listed about a hundred more, but

Creative Homework: Places to Google (or Visit!) for Inspiration

Urban Cowboy, Brooklyn, New York, and Nashville, Tennessee

Bunkhouse Group, Liz Lambert, numerous locations

Freehand Hotels, Miami, Chicago, LA, New York

The LINE Hotels, LA, DC, Austin

This Old Hudson, Hudson, New York

Hewing Hotel, Minneapolis, Minnesota

Lokal Hotel, Philadelphia, Pennsylvania

The Jennings Hotel, Joseph, Oregon

Farmhouse Inn, Sonoma, California

Camp Wandawega, Elkhorn, Wisconsin

Postcard Inn on the Beach, St. Pete Beach, Florida

1 Hotel, Brooklyn Bridge, Brooklyn, New York

Jessica Helgerson Interior Design, Portland, Oregon

Mountain Modern Motel, Jackson Hole, Wyoming

Jersey Ice Cream Company Design, Brooklyn, New York

Kaemingk Design, Portland, Oregon

Rockwell Group, New York, New York

The Beach Lodge, Hollywood Beach, California

TruexCullins Architecture + Interior Design, Burlington, Vermont

Graduate Hotels, numerous locations

Bobby Hotel, Nashville, Tennessee

Joanne Palmisano Design, Burlington, Vermont

Curio Collection, numerous locations

Annette Joseph's La Fortezza, Tuscany, Italy

Moxy Hotels, numerous locations

Main + Mountain Bar & Motel, Ludlow, Vermont

Before

DESIGN THOUGHT PROCESS: REINVENTING TO MAXIMIZE PERSONALITY

Just because the space was a tiny check-in lobby doesn't mean it has to *stay* a tiny check-in lobby. When property owners Eliza and Justin called Joanne, they had just purchased (almost by accident) an outdated 1960s motel, the All Seasons Motel, at a real estate auction in Ludlow, Vermont (they didn't think they would be the highest bidders, but the place was so dire that no one else wanted it). Joanne walked into the place and saw the little lobby, the overgrown front yard, and the manager's office and suggested blowing out the wall to the manager's apartment (which was not being used) to create a bar and to redo the front yard to create a useable outdoor patio. This way, they could turn the check-in area into a bar.

With a few measurements and a concept design in hand, this young, hip couple was excited to give it a go. The space they created was an immediate hit, and it garnered national attention within the first few months of opening. Justin, a mixology expert, was really excited to make the bar into a fun space. He really loves hexagons, so Joanne designed a bar with oversized hexagon tiles, simple painted wood, and some cool, affordable but unique light fixtures. With retro green barstools, salvaged doors, porch posts, and many vintage finds, the place is filled with character. It's proof that cool design does not have to be expensive.

After

this sample introduces you to people who have unique and gorgeous designs as well as fun and inviting websites, marketing strategies, and social media engagements.

As you peruse the various sites, pick out an idea or two from each that you like and that could work for your space. See what marketing and customer service ideas they've employed, and take notes! Don't let this homework project overwhelm you; it's meant to inspire you and to get your creative juices flowing. Remember, even small changes can make big impressions.

Reality Check—Real Costs and Expectations

Reality check here . . . most of the projects you see on reality shows are not based on "real life" costs. Put another way, things always cost more than you think they will. An important question to ask yourself is: Will a redesign bring in more guests and more money? The answer will be somewhat of an educated guess, but one you need to seriously consider. Get yourself in a neutral space and run a bunch of numbers (real ones) to see what the best balance is for you. If you have a large project, it's truly best to hire professionals. Not only will they do things to code, but they will give you a realistic price of what things will cost. If it is a small cosmetic change only, then your job will be much easier: a can of paint, some new bedding, removable wallpaper, some new light fixtures . . . easy peasy!

You have to figure out what you can spend, what you want to spend, and what is realistic. It's hard to keep emotions out of this number, but you should try, especially if this is an investment property—you actually want to make money from it—so don't put yourself in a pickle. Go in with your eyes wide open and have real expectations of the costs. If you're losing guests due to your current situation, you may have to go for it.

The cost of your renovation will depend on the size of your project and your local codes and regulations. If you're doing major renovations, you may have to bring your whole building up to commercial codes (sprinkler systems, smoke detectors, and so forth). If your property is a residential building, then you may be able to keep to residential codes and regulations. Regardless, if you are contemplating swapping the location of electrical outlets, updating the plumbing, replacing the flooring, or removing a wall, then it's time to get the professionals involved! Labor will always be a big cost, unless you're doing the work yourself. If you have the skill (except on the tasks that have to be done by a licensed professional), then get to work. If you're truly on a tighter budget, then doing as much work as you can yourself will be your biggest budget-saving item.

The Basics

Common sense . . . where did it go? Sometimes we just need to ask ourselves this question. You may want to roll your eyes when you read some of our common sense ideas, and we get it. But amazingly, after staying in who knows how many rental properties and hotels across the country and abroad we have found that what might seem so simple, so obvious, and so damn basic, is too often forgotten or deemed inconsequential. It's the little things that matter. Get those right and you're off to a great start.

Before you even get into what is so special about your property, you need to get the basics right. When Joanne sits on a square toilet seat (usually in Europe), she just thinks, "What were you thinking? This is not the natural shape of my butt!" When Rosanne is punching her brick-hard pillow, she questions, "Really, is this the only pillow option? Maybe I can roll up my sweater and sleep on it." From design to marketing to customer service, it truly is the little things that matter—including the shape of the toilet seat and softness of the pillow.

Many places we have stayed at are "almost" perfectly wonderful and we had a lovely time, but a lack of attention to the basics let us down. These hardworking owners and managers probably have no idea that their square toilet seats and rock-hard pillows are affecting their customers' overall experience. As an aside, this is why great customer service is so important: guests have the ability to overlook the little things, most of the time, if the host is kind, thoughtful, and authentic. But your business will be better served if a customer doesn't have to overlook anything in the first place. As you go through this book, you will see all the many opportunities you have for enhancing the details of your rental and your guests' experiences.

Facts and Stories

Just because a basic item was once there it doesn't mean it still is. Joanne and her husband recently bareboated (rented without captain or crew) a catamaran sailboat with six other friends. They were sailing off a French island in the Caribbean and guess what was missing? The wine bottle opener! That's right. Plus, to add to their "hardship," there was only a very tiny French press that made only two cups of coffee. Hello, the boat sleeps eight! It was not like they could run to a store and buy these minor items—they were sailing out in the open ocean. So they had to use a pocket knife to open their glorious bottles of French wine (clever survival trick) and had to make four different pots of coffee every morning. The boat may have once had a wine bottle opener and a larger coffeepot, but at some point they went missing. As this example illustrates, it's important to get the basics down and then double-check each time to make sure the basics are still there. Obviously, sailing in the sunny Caribbean and having to open their wine with a pocketknife was not really "roughing it," but you get the point.

Before

DESIGN THOUGHT PROCESS: RUNNING THE NUMBERS ON THE FLOOR

This townhouse in Stowe, Vermont, is part vacation home for the owners and part vacation rental. Its bland interior wasn't helping its online presence and meant it was lagging behind other competitve rental properties in town. It really doesn't take much to remove a non-load-bearing wall and really open up the space, which is what Joanne did here. Removing the wall between the dining and living room areas, and rearranging the kitchen to include a large island, really opened up the place (and who doesn't love sitting around an island?).

The owner also wanted to change out the flooring, but Joanne asked him to wait because she knew that the other changes would breathe new life into the floor and she felt the cost associated with it was not worth it. Once the walls were updated with gorgeous salvaged wood with a whitewash, a new modern chandelier was hung, and a reclaimed wood farmhouse table and vintage rug were added, the floor looked a lot better. Don't be in a rush to pull everything out—see how your choices affect each other before you decide to make major, expensive changes.

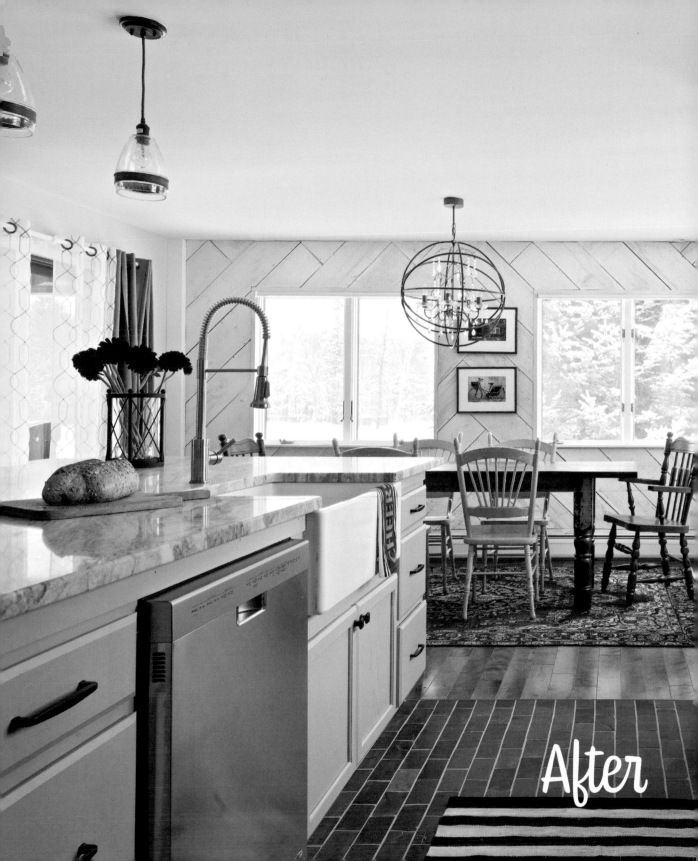

After

Chapter ❷
Design Matters

We're so excited to start chatting about design! The many sections in this book are intertwined, so don't just read one portion, shut the book, and go shopping or tear down a wall. Go through the whole book before you start your redesign. You will see that, just like design, everything should flow and every item should complement each other. Many of our design ideas consist of reusing, recycling, going eco-friendly, and paring down. This chapter introduces you to ideas for design in the form of organizational best practices and budget-friendly advice. But most important, it gets into the details of the design—the little ways you can use design to communicate with your guests and to provide them with comfort and customer service.

Your Design Binder

As you start to plan any redesign or renovation of your rental property, you should begin by creating a Design Binder for your project. This binder should have sections for finishes, fixtures, and furnishings as well as sections for resources and items that you will be using for your Guest Binder (see page 147). Things might start to get a little crazy with all the different sections, selections, and specifications, but you will soon start to find your inspiration.

It's hard to believe that this room used to be a storage space! Now this kitchen, the farmhouse at Mad River Barn, shows just how creative you can get with salvaged and reclaimed materials.

Sample Design Binder Sections

- **Project contacts** (your architect, builder, contractor, and building code offices)

- **Inspirational pictures** (tear sheets from magazines, web images, anything that catches your eye)

- **Overall design concept** (your overall plans and original drawings)

- **Worksheets** (the homework from this book)

- **Budgets and copies of the bills** (so you can reference them for quick access)

- **Finishes** (ideas for paint colors and sheens, wallpaper, stains, plaster, tile, stone, and wood)

- **Fixtures and plumbing ideas** (kitchen and bathroom)

- **Lighting** (subdivided by room)

- **Furnishings** (subdivided by room)

- **Bedding**

- **Bathroom accessories**

- **Design notes** (notes of every meeting, decision, and changed order)

- **Notes for your Guest Binder**

- **Marketing ideas you like**

Joanne loves using large three-ring binders and private Pinterest pages for each client, and Rosanne is all about doing things on Google docs (with a paper binder for magazine cutouts and the like). Choose which method of organization works best for you. When you see an idea you like (light fixtures or cabinetry, for example), save a copy of the photo, the information on how much it costs, and the page that lists its specifications. When you see bedding you love, put that info in the bedding section of the Design Binder. Start putting all your research, notes, and inspiration pictures in one place. When possible, keep tiny, real samples of finishes in a front pocket. Okay, you have your computer, your pen and pencil, your Design Binder, some scissors and tape, a large cup of joe, and a box of Girl Scout Cookies. You are ready to start.

Timelines

When undertaking a renovation or redesign, it pays to be savvy when it comes to timelines. We have seen projects come to a halt because an essential item wasn't ordered on time, or was back-ordered with a promise to arrive by a certain date. Be realistic about time: you would much rather have a sink sit in your garage for four weeks than have a plumber go away to another job because you didn't have it ready and available when it was needed. These timing mistakes can cost money not only in the short term but also when your renovation goes on longer than you thought and you lose estimated rentable days.

When you look at a product, make sure you get the specifications as well as the timelines for delivery and installation, and then always add some buffer. We like to add three to four weeks to be on the safe side. For example, installing plumbing fixtures may not happen until day 17 of a project, but everyone needs to know before day one what those products will be so they can lay out everything according to the specifications. You will want to know the ordering timeline so that the items will be there well in advance of when they need them—so no one is waiting for them. There are numerous examples of timelines for various projects that you can find online; a quick search will help you find what your project could hypothetically look like. Obviously, every project is different, but we think it is helpful to under-

stand how long things should take and in which order things usually happen. If you're doing a bathroom renovation, just search for bathroom renovation timeline and pick one that best matches your project to use as an example.

All the photos in this book serve multiple informational purposes. Not only do they demonstrate remodel and renovation ideas, they also suggest marketing opportunities. As noted in an article on VRBO titled "You Could Increase Bookings with Amazing Photos," you need to stage your photos. In the dining room photo of the 1980s Sonoma vacation rental, you can see we added a beautifully styled vase of flowers. Although this room had already been transformed into a modern, sophisticated, and special place worthy of many superb dinner gatherings, the vase of flowers really gives the photo its wow factor—it draws the eye of potential guests who are looking through hosting sites for rentals in the area. Where can you add a little styling? A throw blanket on a bed, a beautiful bar of soap in the bathroom, throw pillows on the couch, a canister of wooden spoons in the kitchen, a potted plant in the entranceway. . . .

This vacation rental in Sonoma, California, was built in the 1980s—all white, sterile, and bland. How do you make this an Instagram- and Pinterest worthy rental with a limited budget? Rosanne came up with design ideas that were cosmetic (to save money) yet bold enough to make a statement in a town full of vacation rentals—from a 75-percent-off clearance chandelier (it was pink but gorgeous . . . Rosanne couldn't believe the client said yes!), a European-style peel-and-stick wall mural, and a mix of modern (but romantic) table and chairs from a flash sale furniture website and voila!

She knew the timeline on this project would be easier to manage because the work was mostly cosmetic. She just had to make sure she had the chandelier there and ready for the electrician to install, and that the removable wallpaper was on hand so the carpenter could help her put it up. The rest fell into place. As she often does, she kept copies of the bills and materials in her Design Binder, just in case. If they ever had an issue with an item, they could easily find the contact information of the person who provided it.

Discounts and Deals

You've established your budget, and now it's time to stick to it. When design-ing your space, don't be afraid to bargain hunt a little. If your budget is snug, but you want a great design, look at all the avenues that are open to you—such as seconds in a tile shop, returned items at a furniture store, closeout sales, or a scratch and dent at an appliance store.

Bargain hunting is second nature to a lot of people, but bargain hunting for finishes and fixtures is a little different from bargain hunting for décor. Even so, the concept is the same. You just need to find your favorite shops that sell high-quality products. Look for reputable places that architects, design-ers, and contractors visit often. Sometimes they have extra of something, or a piece that was returned because it was the wrong size or shape but in perfect condition, or something that has been discontinued. Just ask nicely if they have anything along those lines.

We're not too ashamed to walk into a lighting or furniture store and ask if they are selling any floor models—you know, the stuff that is on display in the store and they change out by season or year. Ask to get on their list when they change it out. Or to hit up a carpet store and ask for remnant pieces of nice carpeting (usually at a deep discount price) and have the edges bound to create an instant area rug—this binding can run from a dollar to three dollars a foot.

Rosanne got a Viking stove at a scratch-and-dent sale. Once the stove was in the cabinets the dent wasn't visible. Joanne once bought a large commer-cial refrigerator for $600 at a recycle center nine months before the project even needed it. Why? Because the retail cost of that refrigerator was around $8,000, and no way in h-e-double hockey sticks was that in the budget. So when an opportunity presents itself, don't be afraid to grab it. It never hurts to ask if you can get a discount. The store may be having an online special, a 20-percent-off coupon may be available, or they might be willing to pass along their designer/builder discount rate—if you're doing multiple projects you may be able to get this rate; just ask.

And let's not forget the discount days at Goodwill, or secondhand shops, or your local online sources (Craigslist, Front Porch Forums, and the like) for leftover or used materials and products. With any secondhand material or product, there is some good advice for do's and don'ts. We are very careful to clean items well before bringing them into any location, and we are hesitant to purchase upholstered items unless we know how it was handled (heat cleaned) or we know the cleanliness of the house it came from. Even then, we clean things well. Depending on what you buy, how you clean it can differ. Be aware of what you're buying and if it is a risk or not for your location. Once properly cleaned and prepared, these materials and items should not only add character to your vacation rental but usually save you money, if you have the time to search them out.

That said, make sure that any secondhand or slightly damaged and discounted items flow with your design concept and have good long-term value. A discounted rug that has an obvious stain really isn't the best long-term solution, for example. Quality over quantity is our mantra, and it should be yours, too. Throughout this book, there are designs that range in cost from a few hundred dollars to a few thousand to complete property overhauls. But even the complete overhauls were undertaken with a keen awareness of their budget, and they incorporated materials and layouts that accommodated their upgrade needs within their "per room design" budgets.

Facts and Stories

In October 2018, *Lodging* magazine published a story that made eight travel predictions. The seventh entry was titled "Experiences." "*Experience* is a buzzword that won't go away anytime soon. Almost two-thirds of travelers (60 percent) now value experiences more than material possessions. Next year, travelers will continue looking to eat, sleep, and shop in ways that will create lasting memories. Nostalgia will also come into play, with 42 percent of travelers planning a trip that makes them feel like a kid again, so expect to see more ball pits and bouncy castles for adults." Knowing this information, think carefully about how your four key elements (functionality, simplicity, design, and authenticity) will tell your story and create experiences for your guests.

Before

DESIGN THOUGHT PROCESS: REACHING OUT TO FIND A DEAL

In this total renovation of a vacation house, Joanne contacted the local lumber mill and asked if they had any leftover flooring from a project or anything they were trying to get off the floor. It turned out they had some character maple, and they sold it to her at a deep discount just to get it out of their warehouse. The real maple flooring is gorgeous and was less expensive to install (including sanding and sealing) than a faux wood product. The couch was a return from a furniture store, and she got it at cost. The chandelier she picked up with a designer discount, because she used the same lighting store for all the lights in the house. These are just three examples of the many dozens of discounts and deals Joanne picked up for this vacation rental house.

After

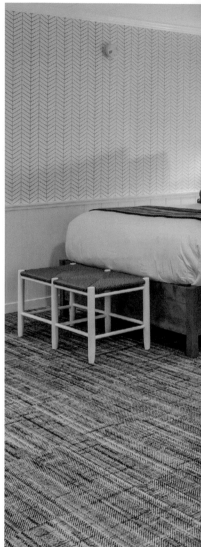

Before

DESIGN THOUGHT PROCESS: CREATING A BRAND THROUGH DESIGN

Joanne has been designing changes at Basin Harbor Resort and Boat Club, in Vermont, since 2014, slowly transforming their 73 cottages and dozens of buildings and rooms to better reflect who the owners are. This five-generation, family-owned resort and boat club (think *Dirty Dancing* but way cooler) has some amazing history and an enviable location on the shores of Lake Champlain. Combining their history, their Audience Profile information (returning families over many generations; traditional cottage styles combined with old-world elegance; lakefront adventure; outdoor sports such as swimming, golf, boating, and tennis), and the location, Joanne has put together a design that allows each space to feel unique while giving them some consistency across the property.

In this guest bedroom, Joanne changed the layout while adding character and layers with wainscoting and wallpaper. The décor is now reflective of the area and the modern, clean lines of the amenities are a big hit with guests. It's all been carefully thought out: good bedside lighting (which includes a way to charge a phone), an alarm clock with USB outlets in the top, great mattresses, a place to set down luggage, extra space between the beds, a large mirror, and vintage nautical signal flags that have been shadow boxed.

After

The Four Key Elements

When thinking about a design concept that works for you, your space, and your budget, consider four key elements. These remain the same no matter the size of the property or your budget.

Functionality

Look at ways to create designs that help your guests more gently occupy your rental. As a result, you will keep the wear and tear of your place to a minimum. Examples abound. For instance, most people throw their suitcase on the bed because it's there and it's an easy thing to do. But you don't want folks to put their dirty suitcases on your white linens! So make it easier for them to put it somewhere else, like an open luggage rack, an open closet with a bench, or a bench placed at the foot of the bed. Not only do these functional details make it easier for your guests to unpack, but it helps you keep your bedding cleaner and longer-lasting. Do the curtains provide actual privacy at the windows, or are they just decorative? Is there an easy way to bring them up and down? Is your shower curtain placed well so that the liner stays inside the tub or shower area? Do you have a good-looking mat by the door for shoes? The list goes on and on.

Simplicity

Look at each room. Does it have no more or no less than it needs? Don't add décor for the sake of it. If it doesn't have meaning don't add it. Clutter means more things to clean or even have stolen. Of course, you don't want the place to look stark (unless that is the look your guests might like), but don't overdo it.

Design

Is your space well designed? Was the building thought out as a whole? That is, do the rooms and public spaces feel like they belong together? Is the lighting comfortable and inviting? Do you get a sense of place and local character? There is nothing worse (okay, there are a lot of things worse, but this is one of our fingernails-on-a-chalkboard moments) than going into a place and encountering a dozen different styles. For example, the lobby is industrial, the guest bedrooms are cottage style, and the bathrooms are mid-century modern. Too much! When nothing is consistent, then your guests will not feel grounded to a specific place. We are sure you can think of a place that subconsciously feels wrong—you know—the restaurant you go into that is beautifully styled in a traditional fashion, but then you head into their bathrooms to find white wainscoting, pale green walls, and dried flowers. Did we suddenly jump through a wormhole and land in a country cottage? Nothing is wrong with any of these styles, and in the right location they can all create stunning spaces. And we are all for an eclectic design, but let's be clear—eclectic design style does not mean each room has a different "specific" style. Eclectic design doesn't mean throwing out all the rules. Rather, an eclectic design means mixing styles and periods in one space through the use of textiles, colors, and shapes. Understanding these distinctions in design will help you create a space that flows with your brand, building, and style.

Authenticity

Does the space feel "real"? Does it feel like it belongs? Do you feel good about being there? Local materials, recycled products, quality bedding, décor touches that have meaning to the city or town you're in . . . all these things add to the authenticity of your lodging and keep your guests coming back for more.

These four key elements combine to tell a single story. They convey to your guests the experience of your property, your services, and your surroundings. The processes for how guests book, plan, experience, and share their trips is very different from even just a few years ago. And this is where the power of your own story and personality can create a competitive edge. Be you. Be honest. And most of all, *be fun*.

After

Before

DESIGN THOUGHT PROCESS: ADDING LAYERS AND TEXTURES

This beautiful staircase railing at Bear Mountain Inn, located in Waterford, Maine, was lost within a sea of outdated wallpaper and a bland carpet. Joanne wanted to keep the charm and character of the space, while giving it an updated and more modern look. She designed the custom wool carpet in black, gray, and white (with many carpet companies, if you have a lot of square footage to cover, they will change the colors of a pattern for you). She also asked the building team to add some custom wainscoting to the walls (which they made with plywood and trim pieces). The wallpaper is textured, giving another layer to the space.

Notice how the rug on the staircase does not go all the way to the edge like it did before; and how part of the wood, painted white, now shows. The result is a bold contrast between the carpet and the wood railing. Now, guests can't miss the charm of this original feature from the 1800s. Meanwhile, they enjoy the clean lines of the modern carpeting and wall finishes. The only décor this space needed was a little greenery for a pop of color. This inn is filled with transformations, but this area remains one of Joanne's favorite spots. Why? Because it shows how you can restore a property without destroying its soul. The history and spirit of a property should be respected, and the balance between old and new rests on a fine line. The trick is to know you're restoring a space without taking away its charm, history, and memories. "Tread" thoughtfully.

After

Before

DESIGN THOUGHT PROCESS:
CREATING AN INTERACTIVE SPACE THAT REFLECTS THE LOCALITY

Now that the large dresser is in between the beds (not only to give this area more room but also to create a little "privacy" space between the two double beds), we have a little room to play. Two faux leather chairs and a table (it's the same table, before and after, painted white) make a great seating area to read, relax, or play a game. The benches at the end of the beds can be pulled up to the table as well. After collecting all the vintage nautical signal flags, Joanne found a large poster that listed the meanings of each flag and placed it above the table. The floor lamp doubles as a charging station. The picture in the coffee nook is of sailor knots, so Joanne hung pieces of rope off the frame for guests to practice making their own knots. Guests are not just staying in a nice room, they are enjoying an experience that reminds them they are in a room near the water at Basin Harbor Resort and Boat Club.

Before

DESIGN THOUGHT PROCESS:
TURNING TWO OUTDATED SPACES INTO ONE AWESOME DESIGN FEATURE

Removing a wall (even a structural wall) may seem daunting. But don't assume it's out of the question—your structural engineer will tell you which beams you need to keep or what headers need to be added. This is Joanne's third project in Stowe, Vermont, with a client who buys properties that need a little love and fixes them up for vacation rentals. He gives Joanne free rein of the design (she loves it) as long as she stays within his budget. This space had some amazing character but uninspiring finishes. By removing the wall, they were able to create an extra-large kitchen-dining space.

She gave it an old-world European feel by playing off the ceiling beams. The builder made the custom open cabinets (which are an affordable alternative to semi-custom closed cabinets), reused some of the base cabinets, and created a countertop using 2-by-2-foot tiles. The same tiles were used for the backsplash. Adding a vintage double-bowl, double-drain sink (a serious wow factor in the room), rewiring the chandelier, and putting in a local maple floor has made this room the heart of the home. This is where guests will hang out at the table and chat through the night. It looks like a large project, but for less than $10,000 (not including the new appliances) this room was redone. (And the structural beam is still there, just hidden in the frame around the refrigerator—clever, we know!) This rental house sleeps 12, meaning it's an investment that will pay for itself very quickly. If we had left the room as is, it's doubtful this property would rent as often as it does now.

After

You Had Me at Hello! First Impressions Matter

You don't get a second chance to make a first impression. According to *Inc.* magazine, humans make their first impression in 50 milliseconds (yes, milliseconds). And with your short-term rental property, your guests engage in numerous first impressions: online when they search, when they book, when they arrive, when they walk in the door, and when they check out. Every first impression is an opportunity for you. You want to make sure you are thinking about all these impressions and how they will help you secure a rental booking in the first place, then encourage trust throughout the rental experience, and then generate repeat business. In this chapter, we emphasize the design part of first impressions; in the next chapter we explore ways to influence the other first impressions of your guests through the reservation process, your online/mobile presence, customer support, communications, and more.

When a guest drives up to your place are they filled with joy? When they park their car and open the front door are they excited? Their first impression will set the tone for their whole stay. Maybe you don't have that much control over the front of the building (your property could be in a townhouse building or a condo complex or an apartment building). If so, think about what you *can* do, such as paint your door, spruce up your patio, and add plants, a bench or chair, or cute signage. Little things matter.

A First Impressions Checklist

How does the front yard look?

Is the front door easy to see? Is it lit up at night?

Does the entrance have a wow factor?

Is it clean?

Is it bright?

Does the entrance have space for guests to set their stuff down?

Does it match what your photos showed online?

Is there helpful, welcoming signage (nothing negative)?

Is there a pretty and convenient Guest Binder?

Have you left a personalized note?

Have you put your best foot forward?

If you can't say yes to all of these . . . keep working.

Cheerful, charming, and creative . . . those are the three Cs Rosanne would use to describe this project she did in Sonoma, California. With a budget in mind, the transformation of this front door is outstanding. It's larger than the old door and the soft pink really pops off the white. Want to catch someone's eye online while they scroll through hundreds of listings in your area? Add some pops of color. Pink doors, red flowers, and a five-dollar garage sale red wicker chair will help! What are some items or colors you can add to make your photos pop? When you did your research of your area, did you see what was renting the most? What did their front door look like? You can get a feel for what folks are looking for in your area by reviewing the most popular listings and by studying the photos that are used the most on their social media accounts.

After

ROCK YOUR RENTAL

Before

DESIGN THOUGHT PROCESS: KEEP THE CHARM, LOSE THE KNICKKNACKS

It was only a couple of weeks after Julie and Brian Sullivan purchased Bear Mountain Inn, an 1800s-built property in Waterford, Maine, when they picked up the phone and called Joanne. They had seen her work at Mad River Barn, in Waitsfield, Vermont, and loved it. Julie and Brian loved their newly acquired property and the bones of the buildings, but they knew that they had to change the look and feel of the décor and to do some extensive repairs and renovations. With hundreds and hundreds of stuffed bears filling the rooms (not to mention the dozens of bear pillows, bear artwork and, yes, bear toilet paper holders) there was a need to purge. Joanne, Julie, and Brian worked together to come up with a plan that not only stayed true to this historic forest and lakefront property but brought in modern-day décor and conveniences for today's traveler.

Joanne wanted to keep the charming paneled walls but lighten up the ceiling by adding tongue-and-groove paneling, painted white. They turned the underutilized glass shelving unit and bookshelf into the visual focal point in the room. The bear, now out of reach of little hands, is a statement piece and is not tucked in the corner as it was before (nobody puts Baby in a corner).

The room now flows better with the half wall gone, and the space feels much larger as a result. The furniture is more modern too, and its placement invites guests to enjoy a cocktail while playing games by the fire. The colors in the woolen area rug tie all the pieces together, including the custom-made, extra-large blue leather ottoman (made from old doors). Overall, there are a lot fewer knickknacks—just interesting pieces that engage the guest: a map of Maine, games, books, a TV, and a fireplace. The result is a more open, airy, and welcoming spot for guests to enjoy, and one that photographs beautifully for their website. Talk about a great first impression.

Your Canvas—Starting from the Back

What we mean by canvas is the backdrop: the walls, floors, and ceilings of your property. This is where you can get a *huge* bang for your buck, especially if you are willing to put in a little sweat equity. We have turned dark living rooms into bright spaces with the magic of paint. We have given character to bland bedrooms with custom peel-and-stick wallpapers. We have enhanced the texture of dining room walls with painted reclaimed wood. And we have added fun to a bathroom by painting wide black-and-white stripes on the walls. These are just a few examples of what we have done to change up the "canvas" of our spaces.

These areas are large and can have a big impact, so start with the canvas (the background) and work your way forward. You can lighten or darken a room (giving it a specific mood and character) with just a change of color. Determining your property's style, be it beach cottage, city farmhouse, bohemian gypsy, speakeasy, botanical, modern, contemporary, country, or whatever you come up with, will influence the type of canvas you create. Look back at the inspiration pictures in your Design Binder or your bookmarks online, and reflect on what the canvases of the spaces you love the most look like.

Yes, a pillow may inspire you. Or maybe that must-have vintage rug is the centerpiece of the room you envision. That is all good. But remember, when you can, start from the back and work your way forward. Like a still life painting, you start with the backdrop and then you add the vase, flowers, and subtle shades of color all around.

If you have a townhouse, condo, or apartment that has trim work or finishes (floor, carpet, and the like) that lack charm but can't be changed, then work around them. If you can paint, add some color with a datum line (more on this coming up), or add a giant wall-to-wall mural on one of the walls in a room, like in a dining room or above a headboard in a bedroom. Other options include installing painted wood or hanging a rod across the top of a wall and adding some gorgeous textiles that go from ceiling to floor across the room. Textiles help with sound and really add texture to a room.

The great news is that your canvas can be changed with just a few hundred dollars in materials such as paint, wallpaper, fabric, or wood. If you can do the work yourself, that will be it in terms of cost. We're talking dramatic changes for relatively little money. Or if you are doing a major renovation, then start to pick out materials for your entire space, not just one room, and lay them out together to make sure they flow. Does the bathroom floor tile go nicely with the flooring in the living room, kitchen, and beyond?

A Few Ideas for Canvas: Backdrops for Your Walls, Floors, and Ceilings

A faux brick stick-on-wall mural for an industrial look

A rod with colorful/dark/moody textiles hung along a back wall, creating a bohemian look

Painted dark gray and white stripes to create a contemporary and modern look

A wall of stacked wood (cut very short, creating the impression of actual stacked wood) for a cabin look

Dark gray painted walls with a wax-like finish for a moody look

Crisp white walls for a clean and contempary feel

Painted wood walls for a farmhouse style

A large vintage-style mural of a sailboat at sea for a cottage

Plaster walls (embellished with a faux painting technique) for old-world charm

Large floral wallpaper for an elegant-country-estate look

Faux beams added to the ceiling to give it character

Tongue-and-groove ceilings always look great in a farmhouse-style space

Reclaimed wood flooring is a stunning backdrop for any style

Bold, modern linoleum works well in bathrooms and kitchens

Thin bricks (real or faux) look amazing in entranceways

Large black and white tile in a sunroom or kitchen give off an old-world charm

Areas That Paint Can Transform

Walls

Ceilings

Wainscoting/paneling

Trim

Doors

Cabinets

Furniture

To Paint or Not to Paint

Paint is one of the most affordable ways to make drastic and dramatic changes to a space. If you really want to brighten up a space and give it a clean, fresh, modern look, start painting. So how do you decide whether to paint the walls or furniture? We encourage you to stay as true to your comfort level as possible.

Here's an example. Let's say you are working on a rustic cabin in the woods that has wood paneled walls. If the walls are in good shape, then they could stay a lovely natural color. But if they are in really bad condition, or if they are a scary orangey pine, then maybe painting the walls a dark rich green, blue, or gray is the way to go. In this case, you would need to make sure you apply a product that is specific for covering knots, and then use your primer and paint. Don't forget how important it is to prepare your areas for the paint. It would stink if you spent a ton of time painting knotty pine wood walls only to have all the knots bleed through within the year.

What does your canvas look like? The floors, walls, and ceilings are the first things to be designed. It's important that your palette of materials works well together so as to create a nice consistency through the space. When Rosanne designed this modern living room in Sonoma, California, she started with an engineered European white oak wood floor, white walls, and white ceilings. Then she added a giant statement artwork piece, a modern L-couch, large baskets to keep extra blankets, leather chairs, and a geometric rug to pull it all together.

Before

After

DESIGN THOUGHT PROCESS:
DIFFERENT FINISHES FOR DRAMATIC RESULTS

This bathroom renovation, in Sonoma, California, was almost all cosmetic. To save money, Rosanne didn't move the plumbing and, while the shower base was enlarged, the footprint of the room remained the same. Following her overall design theme, modern farmhouse, she added details that gave her a more comfortable and usable bathroom that really makes an impact.

She started by enlarging the shower base to go all the way to the wall. This created an open and airy shower with natural light from the frosted glass window. Contemporary black penny tile in the shower area is both modern and classic. She also found a white wavy subway tile for the walls, and she used porcelain tiles that mimic popular (more expensive) hand-painted tiles for the flooring. In such a small space, going bold paid off. Although we all love glass doors in showers, an affordable alternative is a shower curtain. Here Rosanne used a crisp white shabby-chic cotton with a liner (always use a shower curtain liner). She styled the room with a Turkish towel, a simple bar of soap, a vintage stool, and greenery in the shower itself. Inviting, classic, and bold. This picture will definitely cause potential guests to stop in their tracks as they scroll through listings online.

Facts and Stories

We previously mentioned the term datum line. What is a datum line, you ask? It is simply a consistent line carried through the field of vision. You have no doubt seen this line a lot in design lately. It can be when a wall is painted two different colors—sometimes it is at chair-rail height, aligned with a windowsill, sometimes it is along the top of the wall, and sometimes it is a horizontal break at about four feet. You can use different types of material to create this line to give your room some character, but paint is the truly affordable solution.

We have seen both bold and subtle looks, and frankly, we love both. If your project is in a home that has old-world charm, you may want to go with a light gray and a light pink (that is, earthy tones—like the look of a plaster wall) and have the line be at bar height, about 42 inches. If you're doing a cottage by the sea, you can go bold with a bright blue and a crisp white on top, and have the line be at countertop height. For a bedroom we have seen glorious datum lines that are a little loose in terms of line perfection and feature a darker color as high as 6 feet and a lighter color above that. Pinterest has some amazing pictures of different effects and looks with a variety of colors. Take a look to see which ones appeal to you, but more important, ones that fit with your project.

Before

DESIGN THOUGHT PROCESS:
HOW PAINTING HELPS YOU SEE THE UNPAINTED PARTS

When Joanne first saw this old barn camp in southern Vermont, which she had been hired to help turn into a private vacation home, she was blown away with how gorgeous the bones of the place were. The details of the barn beams now stand proud, because the rest of the wood has been painted a crisp white. This is a great example of how a color contrast can bring drama to a space.

By brightening up the walls, bringing in warm metals, and installing contemporary lighting and furnishings, this small private vacation home, around 1,000 square feet, is now a model of rustic sophistication. Also note the new windows, the window seat, and how the brick was kept as is (just cleaned up). Joanne styled the room with a basket of birch logs, local artwork, a gorgeous throw and pillows, and a Scrabble game. Touches like these help guests picture themselves in the space, and they are important things to consider for your online photos.

After

This close-up shot of a remodeled kitchen in a vacation home in Stowe, Vermont, shows how simply made open-shelving cabinets, plus just a bit of paint, can really add drama to a kitchen. Using a dark gray paint, these pieces of plywood and dimensional lumber (you know, 2-by-4s; 8-by-10s) were transformed into cabinetry with old-world charm. We used the same paint color and lumber to create a shelf above the large backsplash (tile pieces) and the facing for the stove vent. We used very affordable large tile pieces to create the stone look for this kitchen, and we faced the tile pieces with painted pieces of wood to make the tiles look thicker than they actually are. Clever, right? This example shows that you can still create a great design on a modest budget.

Before

DESIGN THOUGHT PROCESS: THE PROOF IS IN THE PAINT

Can we all agree that painting this room was the best decision? Thanks. On the main floor of Bear Mountain Inn, in Waterford, Maine, we converted two rooms into a suite. The floors were already painted in a dull white and gray, but they needed freshening up. So that got a new coat of bright white paint. Then the walls received a coat of lovely calming gray, although the trim was left as is—you just couldn't see it under those blinds and curtains. We added a slimmer blind and inset it into the window. We created a cozy sitting area with an electric fireplace and some quality swivel chairs (with stain-resistant fabric) and a HomeGoods wooden-top table in between.

Other things to point out are the comfy area rug, the plant stand, and the gorgeous wool blue blanket. Note that the bed frame is the same, but we cut off the hip-killing corners at the end of the bed. Sometimes the height of these can visually cut a room in half. Remember to consider what you have first—sometimes small changes allow you to reuse a piece. We included the edge of the bed in the shot so guests could see how the room was laid out—we didn't want to pretend the space was larger than it was. It's now a cozy master bedroom, adjacent to a cute bunk/living room area for the kids.

After

As you can see with this close-up shot of the bedside at Mountain Modern Motel in Jackson Hole, Wyoming, the light fixture serves two beds. Also, on the left side of this bed is a floor lamp next to a leather chair. Another item we like to put in rooms is also shown here: the cube clock, with plugs and USB ports. Having this on the nightstands allowed the TruexCullins interior design team to pick a nice light fixture that doesn't have USB ports in it. If you are not going to use something like the cube clock shown here, then you may want to consider using a light fixture that does have plugs and USB ports. These are easy to find at your local lighting store. Hardware and home goods stores are now selling them, too. If you can't find them locally, they are easy to find online.

Let There Be Light

One of the most underestimated pieces of design is lighting. People laugh at us because we travel a lot with headlamps in our suitcases. But when we rent vacation rental properties, a lot of times they don't have proper lighting for the beds, so we have to use them to read. Or they don't have night-lights in the bathroom, so we have to use them in the middle of the night to get to the bathroom. Instead, wouldn't it be nice to turn on a light switch, and dim it to just the right brightness?

If you don't have the option of installing hard-wired lighting, then think of ways you can add more lighting to a space. The goal is to give your guests plenty of lighting options. Consider both task lighting and decorative lighting, and remember that sometimes a light fixture has to serve in both capacities. Just make sure there is a light switch by the door, so that when your guests arrive they can easily turn on a light. Also, make sure there is plenty of lighting in a bathroom. No one likes to squint while trying to put on their mascara—a serious accident can occur! Lighting doesn't have to be boring. You can have lighting that makes someone smile, captures your guests' attention, or creates a mood. Have some fun with it.

Whenever possible, natural light is best. That means windows. Just remember that when you are designing boutique-sized hospitality lodging and vacation rentals, privacy (and blocking light) is very important. Guests want the *option* of opening blinds or curtains, so make sure you have beautiful, yet functioning, window treatments. Unless you own a chalet at the top of a privately owned mountain, you'll need to do more than put up a single curtain. Window treatments give guests comfort, both consciously and subconsciously.

Make a List of Your Lighting Needs

- Light for outside (with a motion sensor?)

- Light for an entryway (to help guests get their bearings)

- Overhead light (ceiling fixture, especially in a dark space)

- Bedside lights (so someone can read without blinding the person next to them)

- Task lighting (makeup light, kitchen lighting, desk lamp)

- Night-lights (bathroom and hallway)

Facts and Stories

There are so many options for window treatments, drapery, roller blinds, Roman shades, blackout curtains, blackout blinds, sheers, shutters, and more. Even though we joke about how many options there are, you had better think about them very seriously. Do you need insulation for a drafty window? Do you need noise reduction? Is a blackout a must for late sleepers? Privacy curtains for first-level living? Sheers so the sun doesn't blind your guests? Maybe all of the above? Just know that guests don't know your neighborhood and maybe don't want to wave to the folks walking by when they wake up. Make a list of your curtain, blind, and shade needs. Then pay a visit to your favorite local window treatment store so that you can touch and feel your options. Bring some basic measurements (and photos) of your windows. Draw out the measurements, too: inside, outside, trim, and so on. You will quickly get a feel for pricing and your best options.

When it comes to smaller budget-friendly vacation rentals, we are big on inset blinds. As compared to curtains or roller shades and Roman shades, inset blinds take up less room and are easier to clean. When we are working with pull-down roller blinds or curtains, we use a sheer as well whenever possible. This gives guests some privacy but still allows them to enjoy the natural light and to see out. They can close the darker curtains when they head to bed.

Furnishings and Décor

Take a hard look at your space. Seriously, we understand that you love the dried flowers you picked up from your trip to the forest, and the 16 half-lit candles that line the windowsills, and the five charms that hang from the light fixture in the kitchen. But is all that décor adding value, supporting your personality and brand, or is it just clutter lying around making the place look untidy?

Once you've done a purge, you can start to reintroduce your belongings, or better yet, rethink where they go and how they are styled. In many of our projects, we reuse as much as we can (what we don't use we donate). But we place them in a way that is totally different than they originally were. Can you group all your beautiful landscape shots together? Can you put your collection of vases down the middle of the table? Can you create a bar area with all your alcohol paraphernalia?

We know it is often hard to ask other folks what they think, but maybe you can get a friend whose design eye you trust to come over and look around. You don't have to take all the advice you receive, but maybe you will better understand how other people view your furnishings and décor.

Before

DESIGN THOUGHT PROCESS:
GET CREATIVE WITH REPURPOSING

When you're furnishing your boutique hospitality or vacation rental, think outside the box and get creative with what you use. Joanne spied this cart at Barge Canal Market, a vintage shop in Burlington, Vermont. There was also a butcher-block top sitting around as well. She asked if they could cut the top and place it on the cart, and they happily obliged. Now it makes a lovely movable cart in this vacation home kitchen. You can also find items like these to make instant bars, coffee stands, or game tables. What kind of character can you bring in with functional furnishings?

After

Before

DESIGN THOUGHT PROCESS: START FRESH AND KEEP IT SIMPLE

When our friend Cari and her husband Vincent called Joanne to see if she would fly out to Michigan and help them turn an outdated Victorian B&B into an entire house vacation rental, she took one look at the before pictures and jumped on a plane. It seems like a huge transformation, and it is, but the renovations themselves were very small indeed; 99 percent of this room's changes were cosmetic only. By painting the walls a calming gray (the gorgeous old trim was already white but you wouldn't know it because it was covered up) and by adding a few pieces of décor and new bedding, the room was completely transformed. We didn't have a choice but to put the bed in front of a window, but we made it work.

This bedroom proves that serious cosmetic changes can happen in just a few days. In keeping with the building's style, Cari, Vincent, and Joanne kept a hint of the Victorian feel. This was accomplished with the vintage dresser and a new lamp that looks Victorian, and by keeping the décor simple.

The antique marble-top dresser with a mirror was actually reused. It was originally located in another room that was turned into a bedroom featuring bunk beds. As this example illustrates, don't get rid of all your furnishings and décor. Many times they are just in the wrong location, are not styled properly, or can be put together in a different way (or painted). Whenever we can, we reuse what owners already have. If we can't, we either sell, donate, or recycle it. Nothing should be thrown away!

After

Before

DESIGN THOUGHT PROCESS: REUSING YOUR OWN STUFF

This room at Bear Mountain Inn in Waterford, Maine, needed a little love. It was cozy and comfortable, but it could use some pizzazz. Even small changes will automatically make other things look totally different. Changing out a rug, wall color, or bedding can change the look of a bed, dresser, and end tables. Many times, our clients just want to get rid of everything, but we ask them to hold off because we really believe that things can look so different, depending on how they are displayed, arranged, or which backdrop they are placed against.

This antique dresser looks lovely against the old barn wood wall, but it would also look amazing against a wall that was painted a semi-gloss bright white, really making it pop. End tables that once were purple in a kid's bedroom can be given a deep black-and-gray, plaster-looking finish and will be transformed. A 1980s porcelain lamp wrapped in old sailor lines can become a show-stopping artisan piece. Change out drawer pulls, lampshades, and bedding . . . but see if you can still use the big pieces you already own.

After

The bathroom originally had baby blue walls and an outdated light fixture. Now with a reclaimed wood wall and a new light fixture, it flows beautifully with the bedroom. The towel, hung on a vintage barn door pull, adds some extra character to the space.

Okay, now that you have purged, you need to refill the space and make it comfortable. Can you bring back in some of your own stuff? Do you need to paint it or reupholster it? Do you have enough chairs, couches, benches? Make a list of your furniture needs and then see if what you already have can be reused (if you give it a little love). This assessment will also tell you what you need to purchase.

If your budget is tight, then start your search on Craigslist, your local Habitat for Humanity, secondhand furniture stores, and so forth. Chances are you'll find some amazing items, and many times the quality and character of an older piece can't be beat. If you want to buy everything new and you have some money to spend, we recommend you look at the products from quality furniture companies that have eco-brands and design their pieces to last using first-rate hospitality-durable fabrics. We have a few brands we love, and we have listed them in Chapter 4 of this book for you to consider. Just remember . . . comfort is *everything*. Cool looking chairs that are crazily uncomfortable, well that just doesn't work for us. Take time to make sure you are getting comfortable pieces.

Facts and Stories

We often find great furniture pieces at secondhand shops that have a little ding here and a little ding there. The quality of the pieces, however, is what catches our attention. Reusing is always foremost on our minds, because it is a way to help waste less. Buying used is also a way to save money, and the number of pieces we have transformed into vanities, nightstands, bars, and office storage units will surprise you.

Always look for quality pieces (dovetail corners, sturdy real wood legs, and good brand names). Cheap pieces will always look cheap and be cheap. And cheap means you will be replacing items often, which is neither an efficient use of your time nor is it good for our planet. If you have some good but beat-up dressers that work, then give them a really unique paint job (chevron patterns, stripes, dots, patterns, cows . . . well, maybe not cows) that will catch your guests' attention and be a functional part of the room.

Paint is a simple way to give life to outdated wooden furniture. *But please! Please!* Please do not paint antique furniture pieces that have significant historical (and monetary) value. Find out if you have a high-quality piece or not—that is, a collector's item before you pull out the paint brush. Your local antiques store will know name brands as well as the contact information of local and online appraisers. Take the time to find out what your pieces are worth.

Before

DESIGN THOUGHT PROCESS: MAYBE IT IS JUST LAID OUT WRONG

Don't think just because something was placed in a certain way that you need to keep it that way. Just by changing the layout of your room, you can really change up the design. This room felt cut off from the rest of the space just by where the sofa was placed. The sectional's large gray back was the first thing guests saw when walking into this room. But with some position changes of the furniture and some small décor details (including painting reclaimed lumber gray to transform the boring fireplace wall), this room is much more inviting.

Remember, sofas don't need to be pushed up to the wall, but they certainly shouldn't make a space feel confined or be placed to block the flow. Looking at the back of a large sofa is not really appealing, so consider a sofa table, or something that can go against it. Look at how your furnishings are laid out . . . is there a better way to do it? Can changes make the room feel bigger? More welcoming? Easier to transition through?

After

Here in the renovated Mountain Modern Motel in Jackson Hole, Wyoming, TruexCullins Architecture and Interior Design (and Joanne) created a unique and inviting storage space that also doubles as a hangout desk and eating area. The open storage is not only an affordable solution, but it also allows guests to see all their gear. What's more, the placement of the television and desk (on wheels) allows guests to pull out the table and to put the stools on both sides so that they can enjoy a meal together. Creative design that is also very functional is what makes this motel renovation stand out.

Where Do Guests Put Their Sh . . . Stuff?

Seriously, this can be so simple. Yet, at almost every place we stay, we aren't provided with a place to put our suitcases. A couple of luggage racks are a godsend. What's more, you don't want people putting their dirty suitcases on your bed, so give them somewhere to put them: a large bench at the end of the bed, open shelving and benches along the wall, luggage racks, a dresser, or a closet with a bench. We are also big into hooks! Hooks for the shower, hooks for coats, hooks for the sake of hooks. . . . We mean, we really like them.

Today, we lean toward open shelving and cabinetry. We're not alone. Just look at the pictures posted by many chain hotels these days—the shelving is usually open, even beside the beds. This design is not only for ease of use, but also because it helps guests make sure they don't leave anything behind. Have you noticed that most hotels have platform beds that have toe kick space but don't have space under the bed? This is a nice feature if guests are provided with storage elsewhere. But if the room is tiny and there isn't any extra space where guests can store their luggage, then consider providing a platform bed with storage or a higher bed that a suitcase can slide under. Just make sure you keep the space under the bed as clean as you do the rest of the property.

Design Your Look: The Devil's in the Details

Would you put a bear print in a beach cottage? Probably not. But you could put it in a place called Bear Mountain Inn. Would you put jars and jars of shells in a western mountain retreat? We hope not, but you may consider antlers or pine cones. We aren't saying you can't do these things, but some things just make more sense than others. You already have a feeling for the style, location, and surroundings of your home. You've already put together some inspiration ideas that you like. Now you have to match it up with your target customers and make informed decisions from there. (That being said, no matter where you are, business travelers will want a desk, kids would love games, bird watchers would love binoculars, and so on.)

Before

After

The great news is that the old rules of design have really gone out the window—mixing and matching period pieces, combining the traditional and modern, and blending old with new is the current way to decorate. Eclectic and imperfect is in! That said, there is a world of difference between a nicely styled eclectic space and just sh** everywhere. It's important to understand the type of lodging location you have, and which types of elements fit best in it. Do you consider your place a beach cottage, a mountain retreat, a city industrial loft, a historic mansion, a mid-century modern ranch? Okay, you've got that down. Now let's move on to how to make it uniquely yours.

One of the reasons we get hired to help with design renovations on vacation rental properties, boutique motels, and unique hospitality locations is because we are willing to be creative in our design. It doesn't take much, and most of the time it doesn't take much money either. You just have to be true to the place, be willing to take a few risks, and trust that everything else will fall into place.

DESIGN THOUGHT PROCESS: COMING OUT OF THE CLOSET

When budget, time, and space restrictions come into play—basically when you need to turn lemons into lemonade—you go bold. Every single room in Main + Mountain Bar & Motel, a 14-unit motel, had a closet like this. The rooms already felt small, so Joanne decided to open up the closets and give them a face lift. Tongue-and-groove wood (leftovers from someone else's project), painted a lovely green, made up the walls. We added some modern hooks, a reclaimed wood bench (leftover wood from the headboard project), and a mirror (that once hung in the bathrooms). We created not only a gorgeous space on a small budget but also a very functional space as well. When we photographed the space, we styled it with a few belongings so guests could see how to use the closet space.

Facts and Stories

We love to use vintage, salvaged, and funky pieces in our designs. The character of these pieces cannot be matched. We especially love it when our clients send us to Italy to pick out things at antiques fairs and flea markets and then bring them back (oh wait . . . that was just a dream). When you work with vintage and salvaged pieces, it's essential that they are safe for guests to be around. In most commercial properties, vintage light fixtures need to be rewired and certified UL listed, painted wood needs to be sealed, and rusty metal removed. Vintage materials add charm, but be prepared to get them up to code for safety. If you're unsure about a piece, ask your architectural salvage shop experts; they usually know the answer. And if they don't, then they can point you in the right direction, especially when it comes to wood, lighting, plumbing fixtures, doors, building materials, and many paints.

Before

DESIGN THOUGHT PROCESS: DO YOU KNOW WHERE YOU ARE?

By far the biggest decision for this cottage at Basin Harbor Resort and Boat Club, on the shores of Lake Champlain, Vermont, had to do with whether to paint or not to paint the paneled walls. If the paneling had more charm, we would have kept it as is. But it had an orange tint that didn't have a lot of appeal. We chose to keep the ceiling beams their natural wood color so as to preserve the original character. The character of the beams is highlighted even more because they are surrounded by white paint. Joanne found a blank art canvas at Goodwill and painted it with some white, gray, and blue to create the modern ombré-style artwork over the fireplace. By adding some antique finds from the resort's attics and a few select shops, the space was transformed into the charming lakeside cottage that it is.

One of the most important additions we did was add two more windows on the lake side of the cottage. What a *huge* difference it made—not only do guests feel like they are right on top of the lake now, but the amount of natural light that pours into the room is amazing! When you look at the before photo, do you feel that you are in a lakeside cottage? We didn't. This is what we mean when we talk about staying true to a place. Let the character of it shine through while you give your guests the amenities they need.

After

Rosanne is big into entertaining, so it's little surprise that as part of this Sonoma, California, home design she installed gorgeous open shelving. This full wall unit serves as the bar. Stunning handmade tiles, floating wooden shelving, and vintage barware are just a few of the details of this space. This amenity would be a huge hit in any rental that serves those who travel to a town or region that celebrates wine. Having extra touches like these really ties in your property to the personality of your location and enhances your guests' experience.

Make a Statement!

You can easily create, DIY, or buy design details that don't break the bank. Between our own experience, work, and Joanne's more than 265 DIY projects on the DIY Network, we know—for a fact—that anyone can add some fun details that will get noticed without causing a financial crisis (though you might take away a tiny bit from the beer budget).

When decorating, think about what will appeal to your guests. We love using design ideas that we consider interactive—something that will create an emotional response from guests. Whether it is joy, happiness, enlightenment, or something that puts a smile on their face, we are all in! Think about items that folks will look at for longer than two seconds—and actually point at and say, "How cool is that?" How about wall-sized maps of your area, your state, or the country you are in? Or how about a wall of shadow boxes filled with vintage pieces you found in the attic, or from the folks who lived in the house in the 1800s? The following list notes some of the decorating statement pieces we've used and some we can't wait to try out. We hope these ideas will inspire you to create some statement pieces that work for your guests and property. Have fun with it! After all, having some fun is a big reason why we are all doing this.

Besides making interactive statement pieces, think about pieces that will add a pop of color or wow to a room. These are the pieces that get noticed in the photographs on your booking platforms. The competition for guests can be fierce, and you want someone to notice your listing, stop, and then book it. The first thing they will do is look at the photos you post (if they are anything like us). If the listing doesn't appeal to them in about three seconds, chances are they'll move on to the next listing. Notable statement pieces will make a big difference in your booking rate.

The best pieces make a big statement without costing you a lot of money. These statement pieces must also represent useful, well-meaning design additions to your rental. They can't be just random ideas that don't flow with anything else.

Ask yourself, "Without spending a fortune, how can I create wow spaces that will catch the eye of a guest who is scrolling through hundreds if not thousands of rentals online?" Well . . . we are so glad you asked.

Statement Piece Ideas

Peel-and-stick wallpaper or prints

DIY wall mural

Huge painted canvas

Statement photography: that elephant in the room is kinda big!

Hand-painted wall: words, drawings, maps, or something for guests to color in

Graffiti wall

Quilt wall

Botanical wall or table

Maps: one giant map or a bunch of smaller ones together

Mirrors: a very large one or a collection of smaller ones

Museum wall: a collection of historical materials

Nautical wall: a collection of oars, fishing buoys, ship wheels, shells, or driftwood

Wall of frames: bold painted wall with vintage frames

Miscellaneous wall: cutting boards, baskets, pots and pans, or other collections

Printer blocks: make a pattern on a wall

Lighting fixtures: bold colors against a black-and-white room or oversized

Mix-and-match tile floor or tub surround

Painted stair risers

Overfilled bookcases

Old barn door/shutters/trim

Hanging vintage bicycle

Woodblocks as tables

Giant potted tree

Colorful area rugs

Now, you can take it from here . . .

When designing this bar for Main + Mountain Bar & Motel, Joanne started with the vintage green box and worked around that. She found bold green lighting and some porch posts that happened to be green and white (score!) and were cut in half. She then placed the posts on either side of the lights. Together, these pieces make the bar a focal point of the place—this is the first thing guests see when they walk in the front door (oh, and the plate of cookies). The greenery is changed out, depending on the season.

Joanne was the designer for Lawson's Finest Liquids Taproom (and its retail store) in Waitsfield, Vermont. She worked with the owners, Karen and Sean, from the look to the layout to paint colors to types of wainscoting to finishes, fixtures, seating, custom lighting, and more. They had hundreds of decisions to make. In the taproom and retail store they placed a few statement pieces that really stood out, including a commissioned piece of artwork by a college art student, Erin Bundock, an oversized three-paneled piece—what Joanne affectionately calls, Find the Beer Guy.

Joanne wanted an interactive piece of artwork that was like the Where's Waldo books, but that related to Lawson's Finest Liquids, their beers, the state of Vermont, and the life of Karen and Sean and their family. The goal was to encourage guests to try and find specific items in the art, including Sean Lawson, the beer guy. A list below the painting lets folks know what they are specifically looking for: the beer guy, the Sip of Sunshine sun logo, pictures of hops, and more. It's a statement piece that relates to the company and its brand—check; that's unique and interactive—check; that's fun and engaging—check; that stays local and supports a local artist—check; that's beautiful to look at—check!

College art students, tech school photographers and video makers, local designers and artisans, and folks associated with lumber mills are just a few of the people you should seek out to find statement pieces. They may have something ready to go, or they could make something specifically for you.

Joanne had been saving this old barn door (purchased at the ReBuilding Center in Vermont for $100) for two years . . . waiting for the perfect wall . . . the perfect client. When Heather and Andrew, at Mad River Barn in Waitsfield, Vermont, called her for help with their extensive renovation (they hadn't even closed on the property yet), she knew exactly where that door was going. The number of people who have stood in front of that sign and taken their family snapshots, wedding photos, and selfies are too many to count! Create a place where your guests will love taking photos of themselves and tagging you in them. It not only looks great, but it is amazing free marketing.

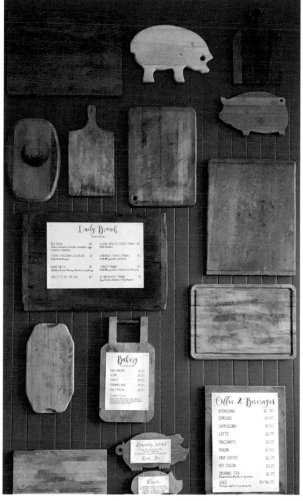

Joanne has a bit of a problem with vintage cutting boards . . . that is, she can't pass one by. Thankfully, she was asked to help with a small renovation of a restaurant/bakery, Vergennes Laundry by CK, in Vergennes, Vermont. She used many of the cutting boards she had collected over the years to create this unique menu board. A menu board does not have to be just a menu board: It can be unique, clever, and functional all at the same time. Think of design as creating experiences, not designing spaces.

If you know a talented artist, then by all means give them a shout and ask them if they would be interested in helping you create a statement piece. You can work with college art students and friends, or you can do it yourself with a projector to create a statement piece of art you like. Trees, stripes, zigzags . . . the options are limitless; and if all you need is a small can of paint, it's very affordable! These trees at Main + Mountain Bar & Motel are a huge hit.

Adding Space from the Space You Already Have

Remember Harry Potter's little room under the stairs? Don't diss it—this could be value added. Of course, there is no need to lock your guests in, but maybe you could take an area like this to create an open space (no door) that is cute for kids to play in. Or maybe you could transform a mudroom by adding beach chairs and umbrellas with a sign that says LIFE'S A BEACH.

We love to create spaces out of almost nothing, and we swear we could write a book about turning closets into mini offices, bunk bed areas, bathroom sinks, full bathrooms, or even check-in desks. Chances are your rental has an unused or underused space. Maybe you could turn it into a cute and cozy nook for napping and reading, or an area for a desk. Can you get creative with the space you already have to offer additional amenities and features to your listing? And don't forget the outside spaces; you can turn these tiny spaces into mini rooms themselves. Areas that you didn't think were special can be extraordinary and can feature into your guests' enjoyment. Imagine an area so cute it must be Instagrammed!

We don't need to tell you that adding a bathroom or bedroom (or even more beds) oftentimes requires a permit, due to city water limitations, septic requirements, fire safety, association rules, and much more. In other words, even though you have all this great extra space, get the facts about what you can and cannot legally do before you bust a move. Or a wall.

Before

DESIGN THOUGHT PROCESS: TURNING CRAZY CROWDED INTO CRAZY AWESOME

This room had nowhere to go but up. These are the kind of jobs Joanne loves. In this space at Bear Mountain Inn, in Waterford, Maine, two rooms shared a hall bathroom (which nobody loved), so it was decided to combine them to create an amazing suite. This suite has a living area with two built-in twin beds (that also serve as the sofa for the TV area) and a lovely bathroom. An old closet is now where the bathroom sink sits. The bed is the same (minus the hip-killing foot posts). With a dramatic wall mural, a barn door slider made from local reclaimed wood, rearranged materials, and cleaned-up finishes, this suite is now a sought-after space instead of the last room picked.

After

Before

DESIGN THOUGHT PROCESS:
TURNING AWKWARD SPACES INTO SOUGHT-AFTER ROOMS

This room is tiny. It really could only handle one twin bed, and because of the angled wall it was hard to see what else we could do with it (except, of course, update the décor). But if you give yourself the opportunity to take a risk and get creative, this type of space can be turned into a winner. Not only did we make this room way more fun, but we were able to get a second bed in there and make space for a couple of chairs. We even added shelves, plugs, and lamps at the head of each bunk, making it easy for kids to hang out and relax and call this room their own.

After

Before

DESIGN THOUGHT PROCESS: ADDING VALUE AND A BATHROOM

This is Joanne's third vacation rental property working with the same owner. She loves the fact that he just says, "Go to town, and here's what I wanted to spend on the project." As an investor, he is all about the bottom line. But when it comes to adding value to the property he understands that sometimes a big investment is required. If he ever wanted to sell this house, which sleeps 12 but had only one full bathroom upstairs (and a scary one in the basement), then he knew he'd have to add a bathroom.

In this master bedroom area there were two large walk-in closets. With some serious calculations and consultations with a plumber and builder, Joanne designed a bathroom for this closet space. Not only did this project add value to the property as a rental, but it added market value to the property if and when the owner decides to sell it. The cupboard doors along the wall were removed to make the space bigger, the window was raised, and affordable fixtures and finishes were installed.

ROCK YOUR RENTAL

After

Facts and Stories

When thinking about bedding for hospitality, we like to have white sheets, pillowcases, and duvet covers—and seriously good quality. Not only are they easier to clean, but they give guests a feeling of cleanliness just by looking at them. Don't just take our word for it. According to *Hotel Management*, a top industry magazine, hotel bedding trends promote wellness and cleanliness; and both hoteliers and their guests equate the color white with cleanliness. But this doesn't mean you shouldn't add a gorgeous blanket at the end of the bed, or some fun pillows. Just make sure that you understand how to clean those items, because they will need to be cleaned regularly. If your rental is your own home and you are enjoying it as your own personal vacation spot as well and you just have to have striped sheets, then make sure they are great quality and look amazing on the bed.

Between the Sheets

The reasons guests are looking at your short-term rental property or boutique inn, motel, or B&B, is because they want a unique place to stay that is not like a traditional accommodation. They want an experience, and although experience is key, they also want a comfortable place to sleep, to lay their head and rest comfortably while on their vacation, business trip, or mental health break. Besides being a place that has character and that creates a unique experience for your guests, you must make sure the actual bed you provide is one of the most comfortable they've ever been in.

The bed frame, mattress, sheets, and bedding are some of the most important items you will purchase for your property. Do your research. If you are buying multiple beds, then we highly recommend that you do business with commercial mattress and quality bedding companies. You can get bulk discounts on amazing products. Besides doing your own research (this includes taking photos of the tags on the sheets and blankets you like while traveling), you can also rely on experts in the field, such *Consumer Reports* magazine, other hotels and motels that get rave reviews for their bedding, and of course, industry catalogs that specialize in these items. Many of the lodgings we work with actually rent their towels and bedding, especially if they have numerous beds. By renting, they get clean sheets and towels delivered and hand off the dirty ones. If you need a commercial-sized washer and dryer, you may want to run the numbers on this versus hiring a laundry service. The small additional fees for using such a service could be preferable to the hassle of doing your own laundry.

The things that you must have in bedding include a mattress cover, for so many reasons, but mostly to protect your investment and to add comfort for your guests. And, of course, you need sheets. Some folks talk about getting rid of the top flat sheet, and in many European places that is the case. They use the cover of the duvet, and they consider it to be the top sheet because it gets washed at every turnover (as it should whether a top sheet is used or not). We are not fans of losing the top sheet. Why? Because if we get too hot and have to take the duvet off, then we have nothing covering us. It may not be much, but subconsciously, even just having a sheet covering us brings comfort. That's our opinion and we are sticking to it! You also need a washable duvet, duvet cover, and blanket (it's your choice whether it is made into the bed or placed at the bottom). It almost goes without saying that you need to provide comfortable pillows: two for twin beds, four for queens, and four (or more) for kings. Place a couple of extra pillows in the closet. This way you have everyone covered regarding soft and firmer pillows.

As for the bed frame, quality counts. No matter what you choose for a bed frame, make sure it is steady, stable, and secure. The trend in the hotel industry these days is toward simple wooden, metal, or custom-made platform beds. Why is this, you ask? There are numerous reasons, but a couple are paramount: they are easier to clean and if the frame goes all the way to the floor, then guests can't lose a sock, a sweater, hat, book, or shoe under the bed (and property owners don't have to deal with the recovery hassle and associated costs). What's more, old rickety bed frames can be noisy and annoying for those who sleep on it.

Before

DESIGN THOUGHT PROCESS: WHEN YOU NEED AN ENTIRE OVERHAUL

Main + Mountain Bar & Motel was once an outdated motel. It is located in central Vermont, and it was unexpectedly purchased at a Sunday afternoon real estate auction. Once Eliza and Justin, its new owners, got over the shock of owning a dilapidated motel, they decided to rock the renovation out of the park. They reached out to Joanne and she immediately fell in love with the lovely young couple and their property. She knew this was going to be a complete remodel job and that it would take a large team to create what it would become, Vermont's first boutique motel. Rosanne started putting together their marketing plan.

Let's be clear, this was a big project with architectural drawings, a fabulous builder, and a designer (Joanne); but the décor, furnishings, and finishes were all budget conscious, from the custom-made bed frame and headboard using local wood to the recycled content carpet to the simple and affordable tile choices in the bathroom. All told, including finishes and furnishings that make a wow statement in design and comfort, the square-foot cost was around $75—unheard of! Joanne kept the design simple to create a modern rustic look. To add to the wow factor, she used contrasting colors such as black, white, and gray with pops of green in the closets, plus lighting, greenery, and other pieces in the room.

After

Before

DESIGN THOUGHT PROCESS: TRANSFORMING WITH DIYS

Yes, guests were actually sleeping on these mattresses on the floor! That is some serious commitment to skiing at Mad River Glen, in Vermont. Here you can see the cosmetic changes at Mad River Barn. The orangish-brown paneling was painted tan, and Joanne made the headboards using faux leather (you can find a step-by-step project tutorial on DIY Network). The artwork was created from scrap pieces of wood that came out of the construction project, an old bicycle rim, and a vintage doily. Joanne and her daughter, Gabrielle, made the pillows from the old wool blankets that were on the old beds (they boiled them and then used fabric paint for the letters and hand stitched the edges). The platform beds were made from the old beams that came out of the building and plywood painted black. Four seriously easy DIYs and this room was transformed.

The carpet squares were from FLOR, and they are almost completely made from recycled material. The rest is quality bedding, including a washable cotton blanket (we like to use blankets instead of throws on the end of the beds, because they are more functional than a small throw). Some industrial-style touches were included, such as the table that is used as a nightstand and the pharmacy lamp. This rustic industrial look is a big hit at Mad River Barn, and the guests are so happy they don't have to sleep on the floor anymore.

After

Welcome to Holly Vault Crossing House in Holly, Michigan. This bedroom in a Victorian-inn-turned-vacation-rental-home didn't need any structural changes. We painted the walls a white color, and we mixed old and new to create a cozy, inviting space for guests. Simple additions, like a yellow painted vintage dresser, a retro vintage lamp, a new boho rug and blanket, a vintage-style (but new) bed frame, and cozy bedding completed the look. Joanne found the print at a secondhand shop while out shopping with Cari, one of the owners of the vacation rental, for only a few dollars. Together, Joanne and Cari spent three full days (and we are talking full—midnight at the store—days) installing all the furniture and décor in the house. Exhausting but totally worth it to get it all done at once.

Our Bedroom List

Quality bed frame

Quality mattress

Mattress cover (foam or cushion for extra comfort and protection)

Quality white sheets and pillowcases

Duvet

Duvet cover

Two pillows per person

Blanket for bed

Extra blankets

Extra pillows

Light for reading

Overall light for room

Alarm clock with plugs on top and USB ports

Place to set suitcases (not the bed)

Luggage rack (or two)

Hangers

Hooks for towels and coats

Privacy blackout curtains, blinds, or shades

Night-light

Other Options

Baby crib and/or small cot

Iron and ironing board

Throw rug by bed (that does not slide out when stepped on)

Fan or sound machine

Before

DESIGN THOUGHT PROCESS: TURN A FLAW INTO A FEATURE

If you have a space with a flaw, think about how you can turn it into a feature. When Joanne saw this room, not only did she see that the layout was an issue, but she felt that the personality the room gave off was awkward, uncomfortable, and outdated (not words you ever want to hear coming from your guests). In short, it was Grandma's attic. She decided to stop trying to make the room what it was not and instead make it fun and inviting. The two built-in beds against the wall are key. The result is a great room for kids or two friends who want their own space. The otherwise unusable wall area now offers more head room, and the walkable space in the room is readily available. Instead of being the last room available at a discounted rate, this space is now a huge hit.

After

Facts and Stories

If you have not seen the world reacting to the plastic crisis, you haven't been paying attention. We are thrilled to see that countries, states, cities, and the hospitality industry are making changes. Of course, we'd like it to move faster. And we cannot even begin to express how we feel about the tiny hotel single-use plastic bottles that get thrown away daily. And these single-use bottles are but one item in a mountain of plastic waste. In the hospitality industry there are plastic bottles for shampoos, soaps, conditioners, and body washes; plastic bottles in the room for drinking water; plastic coffee stirrers, straws, forks, knives, and spoons . . . and this is just the obvious stuff! We are talking an epic plastic crisis. You only need to walk along a plastic-strewn beach once to understand the enormity of the plastic crisis our world is facing. Do your part. Leave out fresh water in reusable glass containers for drinking, use refillable shower amenities, and use real silverware. We like to encourage the use of reusable bottles whenever possible. This matters to your guests, too. Industry statistics and surveys say that some of the most common complaints from guests are single-use plastic bottles and water bottles in the room.

Bathroom Behavior

What?!?! No toilet paper? Seriously. There are times we just have to shake our heads and then go to the grocery store for supplies. Of course, sometimes this is just a mistake, something that got overlooked, but it's hospitality misses like this that get our goat. We're already two people who have "issues" when we travel, and a bathroom that makes us feel comfortable is essential. Take an extra-long look at your bathroom—pretend you're seeing it for the first time. Is everything within easy reach? Is it adequately supplied? Is it a well-lit space where you can put your stuff down? Does it have a clean shower liner? And, finally, is every crack, crevice, and corner clean? (Okay, now we really want you to say that five times fast.)

For us the most important factor in a bathroom is cleanliness—and we mean every nook and cranny. Then lighting. The lighting must be adequate and useful. (We touch on bathroom lighting in the lighting section on page 79—check it out.) As a proprietor, circumstances sometime make bathroom lighting options limited—perhaps the hard wiring is older and can't handle a higher wattage fixture. But when you can control it, you should install proper lighting. That means lighting next to the mirrors and also overhead. There are charts online that will show you everything you need to do to light the space properly, down to where the lighting should be, including the level and distance from the wall. You should also consider installing a night-light for guests who might get up in the night to use the bathroom. It's nice to provide a way for them to find the bathroom without having to turn on an overhead light, or use their phone, a flashlight, or a headlamp. Some great energy-efficient night-lights are available that only turn on when it gets dark.

Whether we're staying in a boutique motel or an Airbnb, here's what we love to see in a bathroom: plenty of large towels, face towels, hand towels, and bath mats. Towels don't have to be just towels—you can fold them beautifully and place them in the bathroom with a lovely piece of lavender on top or you can roll them in a gorgeous basket in the bedroom (if there is no room in the bathroom). Or if you're really tight on space, you can tie a ribbon around each bundle and hang them from a hook. We've seen a number of ways that towels have been used to make a design impression.

Other essential items for a bathroom are a cabinet, shelf, or basket filled with . . . you guessed it . . . extra TP, plus a blow dryer, a bar of soap, a full bottle of lotion, a couple of tampons and pads, a shaver, and a few other bathroom items you are comfortable sharing. In the showers, provide refillable shampoo, conditioner, and body wash containers that are clean and topped off.

Think carefully about counter space/shelving in bathrooms. Your guests need somewhere to put their stuff. The older we get, the more stuff we seem to accumulate (the night creams, the anti-wrinkle creams, the brightening creams, the SPF face creams . . . and let's not forget all our meds!). If the bathroom in your property has little or no room for counter space, creative solutions like vintage stools and a hanging wall shelf come into their own. Create a space for guests to set stuff down, even if it is only 5 inches wide and just big enough to put a toiletry bag. Install plenty of hooks for hanging stuff: drying towels, robes, full-size toiletry kits, and so forth.

Facts and Stories

Tissue, toilet paper, paper towels . . . all these items are necessary and convenient for your guests. But there are eco-friendly ways to provide them that make a *huge* difference in our environment. According to Anthony Swift of the Natural Resource Defense Council (NRDC), "Most Americans probably do not know that the toilet paper they flush away comes from ancient forests, but clear-cutting those forests is costing the planet a great deal." Many "go-to" toilet paper brands use 100 percent trees from virgin boreal forests to create this single-use product. Cuts the size of football fields are happening in boreal forests every two seconds! We mention some eco-friendly products in Chapter 4 of this book for you to consider. Feel free to mention your use of these eco-friendly products to your guests in your materials (print and online). All your guests would like to know you care and that you are trying to make a difference.

Before

DESIGN THOUGHT PROCESS: TURNING UNATTRACTIVE INTO USEABLE

Where do I put down my toiletry bag? That was the first question Joanne asked herself when she was redesigning this space for Bear Mountain Inn. This bathroom was small, and the layout made it almost impossible to be comfortable in it. Joanne redesigned the space to incorporate the underutilized back wall into the design. With some salvaged wood on three sides of the wall, she was able to visually create drama while giving definition for the counter width. There is an open shelf underneath for toiletries and extra items, which leaves lots of space on the counter for the guests to use. This easy design uses a simple wood (you can even use birch plywood as long as it's sealed well), a mirror that was once in another room, and a vintage handle that serves as the hand towel holder. Little touches like these add some personality and character to a space.

After

Our Bathroom Essentials

Hot water (this seems obvious, but it's imperative that the hot water heater can handle the number of guests you have listed in your rental)

Towels

Toilet paper (eco-friendly brand)

Tissues (eco-friendly brand)

Makeup towel (wash towel that can handle dark makeup)

Hair dryer

Shampoo, conditioner, and body wash (in refillable containers)

Thoughtful extras basket (just-in-case stuff like tampons (paper), cotton swabs, Q-tips (cardboard middle, not plastic), comb, nail file, and shaving cream)

Mirror or two

Good lighting

Hooks

More hooks

Shelf or counter space for toiletry bag

Night-light

Lined trash can

Recycle can (if you don't have one in the room)

Impeccable cleanliness (not a single hair, mildew streak, or dirty shower curtain in sight)

After

Before

DESIGN THOUGHT PROCESS: FROM OVERSIZED TO INVITING

This tub was just too big for the space. The amount of hot water it took to fill it up posed a big expense for the new property owners, Cari and Vincent. Still, they didn't want to get rid of the benefit of having a tub when they updated this space in their Michigan Victorian inn-turned-Airbnb.

Joanne put together a design that didn't change the location of the plumbing. Her goal was to create a romantic feel while allowing for storage and a distinctive tub that used less water. The step up to the tub allows for the plumbing to be above the floor—it's an affordable solution to a serious plumbing issue while making it feel like a design element. This is a big change, but if you look carefully at the before-and-after photos, you will see that it's the same space. The transformation is a result of some sweat equity, removing the cosmetic pieces, adding a different tile, creating a built-in shelving unit, and installing an updated tub. Styled with some antique pieces, it still feels very much in keeping with the house.

Before

DESIGN THOUGHT PROCESS: GET RID OF THE AWKWARD LAYOUT

At Bear Mountain Inn, this bathroom with its slanted ceiling felt oppressive. The ceiling slants are a common feature for a house of this age and style, but having a large tub almost at the corner of the angle created a pinch point, which should be avoided. The valance, fabric bench, colorful shower curtain, pink tiles, braided rugs, and angled pink accents were all too much, to say the least. Working with the constraints of the space, Joanne designed the bathroom to feel more open while still keeping it romantic, which was the goal for this room.

The updated flooring and a rustic wood look are in keeping with the historic inn. The modern soaker tub and a smaller shower space with glass door and half wall really open up the space. These elements allow lots of natural light (and lighting) to brighten up the room. The shower feels private but open, and the birch tree wallpaper accent wall provides just enough of a wow to allow the rest of the space to feel calm and inviting. The real bird nests are shadow boxed, lending the room some clever décor without being overwhelming. Simple, clean, inviting, and spa-like . . . just what a guest bathroom should feel like.

After

According to Vacation Rental Pros (vacation-rental-pros .com), an online community for the vacation rental industry, the top six technology amenities that guests look for are the following:

1. Wi-Fi

2. Flat-screen television and DVD player

3. Cable TV or streaming service

4. Universal adapters and/or chargers

5. Tech amenities via an app: custom app for check in/out, local guide info

6. Other smart devices: keyless entry, iPad with custom info, thermostat adjusters, fire alarms with security

Electronics—Today's Techie

Never assume that any electronic piece, appliance, or remote in your rental property is easy to use. Joanne is still trying to figure out how to turn on the DVD player at her home, now that her daughter has left for college and can't do it for her anymore. There is a lot of tricky tech details that your guests must quickly master. In your Guest Binder (more on this to come), include a section for the manuals of all your appliances. Also include a one-page, typed-out, step-by-step set of instructions for how to use each piece of tech: the door lock, fireplace, grill, stove, Apple TV, DVD player, Wi-Fi . . . whatever you have. One page for each piece of tech. At the top of each page should be a clear label. For example: HOW TO CONNECT TO THE WI-FI.

Speaking of Wi-Fi, how-to info for connecting to the Wi-Fi should also be placed somewhere that is easy to see: a nightstand, desk, fridge, and so forth. Strong, reliable Wi-Fi is essential for the success of your rental. Without it you are guaranteed to engender bad reviews, meaning you will miss out on future bookings.

The latest trends in home technology are smart devices like Nest and Alexa. Many devices have cameras, microphones, and features such as remote accessibility. If you install smart devices, it is important that you be very aware of your guests' privacy as well as your own personal security. There has been much debate about security and privacy issues that arise with the use of such technologies. Be aware of these issues, and weigh the pros and cons of each. If you have audio and/or video access to the rental property via these devices, you must let your guests know about this. Further, if you install these systems, you need to read everything about their default settings and understand them. Do not assume the default settings secure your privacy or the privacy of your guests. You may need to change any number of default settings.

The renovated rooms at Main + Mountain Bar & Motel feature flat-screen televisions with DirecTV, keyless entry, and high-speed Internet. The clipboard under the light has the Wi-Fi code info, and the television remote is next to the bed. Side note: The bench was in the room before, but now it is painted black. Also, Joanne recovered it with a more modern fabric that matches the décor in the room. Super simple to do! She didn't want to replace it because it was well made and because it was an easy upgrade.

Before

DESIGN THOUGHT PROCESS: KEEP THE CHARACTER AND ADD MODERN TOUCHES

When transforming this space into a comfortable vacation rental, Joanne decided to keep the old-world feel but to give it a little modern twist. The room had good bones, but they were hard to see with all that dark wood, red carpet, and dingy yellow paint. As part of the redesign, the cabinets were painted a dark gray, and both a modern gas fireplace and a television were installed. Local maple flooring really changed the look of the room, and all the walls were painted a crisp white. When possible, especially in a higher-end boutique hospitality space or vacation rental, use real hardwood floors. They're more work to install, but they always impress guests. The sofa was picked up at our local furniture store (it was a return, so we got a great price) and the chairs came from another resort renovation project. The rug is from an estate sale and the tables are from an antiques shop. All the books are from a used bookstore and a library sale.

After

Cleanliness Is Next to . . . . Well, Cleanliness

At the risk of stating the obvious, cleanliness is essential to rocking your rental. Your rental can look as cool as can be, but if your property is not scrupulously clean, you will be called out on it. Any booking platform you use will provide listings to numerous services. Check the references for all cleaners, see their work, and contact your guests after their stay to make sure the place was up to their standards. Treat your cleaning service well. They are literally the front line of your defense. This is the team that will be taking inventory, and if something is missing they are the ones who will notice it. They represent you and you need to appreciate what they bring to the table—don't treat them like an afterthought. That said, don't assume that the housekeepers know how you like things cleaned, styled, tucked, pinched, or pleated. Clearly lay out your preferences in a friendly Housekeeping Binder, and then walk them through it. Step. By. Step. They are the peanut butter to your jelly, the mac to your cheese, the bread to your butter . . . you get the point. Make them feel that they are a part of your team, and let them know just how much you appreciate all that they do to help you put your best foot forward. If you treat them well, they will be just as eager to straighten out that lamp shade as you are.

We have stayed at places where we could have eaten off the floor. We have also had experiences where we walked into a place, took a look at the level of cleanliness, and walked out to find somewhere else to stay (literally at 2 a.m. we walked out of a place and slept on the floor of the airport instead of being in a room that was just horribly unclean). Oh, and by the way, *neat* is not *clean*.

That said, a guest doesn't want to walk into a rental and be greeted by a smell like bleach, or worse, a spray that you used to cover up the fact you didn't clean. There aren't any shortcuts to a thoroughly cleaned property.

A housekeeping closet is always helpful for your housekeepers, but it's also important that your guests have access to basic housecleaning products. A guest might spill a glass of wine or track in some mud and want to clean up after. You never know. So provide the basics: a mop, broom, dustpan, and cleaning supplies. If you're lucky, you might even host a guest who, like our mom, keeps a place clean and leaves it cleaner than when they got there (we know, you all want her as a guest . . . get in line).

The moral of this story is, again, neat is not clean. Neat, clean, comfortable, and well designed is a gold-star combo.

What Should Be in a Housekeeping Binder

- **Your contact info:** regular and emergency contacts

- **How the beds are done:** how the sheets should be folded, the pillows placed, and so on

- **Cleaning supplies list:** what you have and how to order more

- **Photos of the rooms:** a visual on how the rooms should look when they are ready for guests

- **Checklist of items that should be there:** if something is missing, you can try to track it down with your guest right away

- **How to handle "hot sauced" items:** meaning what needs to be repaired, fixed immediately, or dealt with before the next guest arrives (housekeepers need to know who handles these situations)

- **Lost and found:** how to handle this stuff

- **List of amenities:** make sure your housekeeping team keeps track of the various amenities, sheets, bedding, and cleaning products (sometimes spoons go missing or dish towels accidently get thrown away)

- **Checklists:** provide a checklist that your housekeeping team can use for each check in and check out—they can put the date on the top of the checklist and literally go through it as they clean; all spoons, glassware, dish towels, blankets, artwork, and so forth should be accounted for, and they should check that products are refilled (soap, shampoo, coffee, sugar, milk, and the like)

- **A big thank-you note:** remember, your housekeeping team is key to your success, and without this team, there is no game!

Before

DESIGN THOUGHT PROCESS: DESIGNS THAT LOOK CLEAN AND FRESH

Unless you're really going for a fun and funky look (which is very cool), then stick with classic white for the toilet, shower, tub, and sink. Here in the former All Seasons Motel (now Main + Mountain Bar & Motel) the old bathroom looks tired and dirty, even when it is clean. Sometimes the design alone can make a place feel dirty. Joanne stuck within the constraints of a snug budget and used some tricks of the trade to keep her design in check.

She used large marble-like porcelain tiles on the bathroom walls (not only is the product affordable but larger tiles go down faster, which translates into less labor costs), a shower pan for the floor, a shower curtain and rod (instead of glass), and large dark floor tiles for their ease of installation and a bold look. The hardware store vanity has a great color, a solid top, and clean lines. A simple modern faucet and a fun mirror with a shelf adds character to the bathroom, as do the vintage glassware, bottles, and reusable soap dispenser. Behind the scenes is an energy-efficient water heater (lots of great pressure and plenty of hot water). Add it all up, and this bathroom rocks! And now when it's clean, it *looks* clean.

After

This guest room renovation, done by Rosanne, has given the space a modern romantic feel. There is very little in this room, which makes it a whole heck of a lot easier to keep clean. Less stuff also means that taking inventory is a straightforward process. Whenever possible, leave fresh greens or flowers in your rental; they add a lovely, personal touch. Close-up shots like this can express emotions or moods, more so than full-room shots, so add photos like this to your online gallery when you can.

At Bear Mountain Inn, located in Waterford, Maine, we did some minor renovations in this suite's bathroom. While adding fun wallpaper, a modern mirror, a new sink, faucet, and countertop, we also made a unique holder for the hand towel. Everything in the space balances modern and rustic, shiny and clean.

Before

DESIGN THOUGHT PROCESS: DRAMATIC RESULTS WITH SIMPLE CHANGES

The half bathroom in this Stowe, Vermont, vacation home was given a simple update. Joanne did not move anything: the plumbing, electrical, and cabinetry stayed the same. The room was painted a bright white, and she had the cabinet painted the same color as the cabinets in the living room and kitchen. Then she picked up a beautiful antique sink at an architectural salvage shop and added a modern black fixture. New maple floors, which flow through the rest of the first floor, were continued into the bathroom. The chandelier and the stained glass window were already there, but now they really stand out. She added a hook for a hand towel and some simple décor touches. Elegant, minimal, and classic . . . this half bathroom is now worthy of a photo.

After

Facts and Stories

According to an article in *Hotel Business*, what guests want are a clean and comfortable stay. Over 86 percent say this is the most important aspect of their stay. The most mentioned complaint is smells—they don't want to smell the last guests and they don't want to smell heavy cleaning products or air fresheners. If you clean well, using natural and eco-friendly products, you should be able to solve both of these problems. Guests want the illusion that they are the first guests ever to stay there, with crisp clean bedding, carpets, furniture, bathroom, and more.

Under Promise and Over Deliver

We know we've been saying that you should offer more! But really, what we mean is that you should have a place with personality, keep it clean, ensure it is easy to access, and always put your best foot forward (we don't ask for much). What we don't want you to do is promise stuff you can't control, like perfect weather. What you *can* do is surprise guests with little touches that elevate your offering. We're talking about personal attention and thoughtful gestures your guests will appreciate.

Small gestures can make a big impact and are almost always mentioned in word-of-mouth reports. Sometimes it doesn't take much to add a special touch that makes people happy. You should hold back on sharing/showing some details online for a couple of reasons. First, it's nice to surprise your guests with touches like fresh flowers and a bowl of green grapes, a bottle of wine, some local cheese and crackers, or reusable water bottles with your logo (yes, you should brand your location). Second, you may not be able to provide these touches all the time, for whatever reason—and if something is expected, guests will be disappointed if you don't provide it.

When we think about the places we've stayed we always remember the special touches: the cappuccinos offered to us after hours of hiking in the cold rain in Cinque Terre in Italy; the full pantry and refrigerator of breakfast makings in the studio apartment of the anthropologist's home in Greece; the warm cookies and tea in an inn in southern Vermont; the bottle of wine and cheese left on the counter of our apartment in Montepulciano, Italy; or the fresh flowers and handwritten note welcoming us in a vacation rental in Nashville, Tennessee. We could go on about the treats and touches that have meant the world to us. It doesn't take much to make a seriously good impression on your guests. Hopefully, this list will spur you to come up with some of your own great ideas.

Branding a vacation rental with its own personality is becoming more and more important these days, so why not add special touches (free or for a fee) that are branded, that folks can take with them? How about two coffee mugs with the name of your place on them? Or a reusable grocery bag with an illustration of some local scenery? Other possibilities include water bottles, baseball hats, or flasks with leather patches that feature the name of your place. Simple, affordable, eco-friendly branding materials are readily available—just search online. These items can have even more of an impact if they are locally sourced.

Think about some fun and unique ways you can add touches that reflect your location, your rental, and your style. Even better, you can go the extra mile and ask your guests if they have any allergies or diet restrictions (especially important if your go-to special touch is food).

Some Sample Special Touches for Your Rental or Boutique Hotel

Bookshelves with take-and-leave books and magazines

Large bowl of seasonal fruit

Travel bag with logo/name of property

Hand-painted mini print of the local area

Afternoon tea, coffee, and cookies

Breakfast in a bag (hung on guests' door in the morning)

Cookie platter

Bottle of wine and a cheese plate

All the fixings for a pasta dinner

A book of the area with a signed thank-you message in it

The offer of cappuccino or a glass of wine in the afternoon

Snack food for movie night

S'mores and everything for the fire pit

A small homemade craft that guests can take with them (for example, a beach house might have a shell with a magnet)

In the lobby of Mad River Barn, located in Waitsfield, Vermont, is a take-and-leave bookcase as well as an old ladder that serves as a magazine rack. Guests can bring a couple of magazines into their room to enjoy (or they can sit in the cozy club chair in the lobby and peruse away while watching the action at the front desk). These extra amenities are appreciated by the guests and are used often.

Rosanne's design of this entrance area is simple, elegant, and useful. The special touches of two bike helmets, a blanket, and a wine carrier for a picnic in the park are perfect accessories for the wine country of Sonoma, California. Bicycles, beach towels, picnic baskets, snowshoes . . . what are the items that would be most used in your area? Can you have them available for your guests?

The owners of Main + Mountain Bar & Motel provide a unique service: Guests who order a drink or drinks in advance will have them waiting in their room upon arrival. Invisible bartending is a fun and clever special touch that catches guests' attention—it's room service with a twist. This shot was styled to show off the options available. What are some amenities you can offer, free or for a fee?

Who doesn't love a coffee and tea station? Joanne, who did the interior design for this private vacation home in southern Vermont, made sure there was room for a coffee station. It is such a nice addition to any vacation rental or boutique hotel. Remember to take close-up photos and to post them to your booking platforms. You want to show off the small touches that set your rental apart.

How to Create Good Guests

Creating great guests doesn't happen by accident. There are specific ways to help your guests help you. It begins by showing your guests how much you care about your rental. Meanwhile, you should give them opportunities to take care of your rental, which in turn lessens the wear and tear on the property. Some simple design solutions will help your guests feel like they are part of the family, and that will make for a more pleasant experience for everyone involved.

Signage

We are big podcast listeners, and we listen to many, many vacation rental expert shows. We highly recommend that you start to follow a few. In the meantime, you should know that these experts all agree that no matter how clear you are in your descriptions, binders, contracts, and manuals for how to use your property, many people either won't read your instructions or will totally forget them. This is where signage comes in. We know, it's disheartening to work so hard to put together a beautifully designed rental only to have it ruined by little signs posted everywhere. You might cringe as you put up a sign that says DO NOT FLUSH FEMININE HYGIENE PRODUCTS DOWN THE TOILET in your stellar bathroom. But if you don't put up the sign, you could be effectively sending lots of money down the toilet. Plumbing repairs do not come cheap. Here's the bottom line: The wear and tear on your property can be reduced if you put out some good-looking, kind, yet instructive signage.

At Basin Harbor Resort and Boat Club, on the shores of Lake Champlain in Vergennes, Vermont, Joanne used one of their vintage photos of folks taking off their shoes, added wording beneath it reading: SHOES HERE PLEASE, and made sturdy copies. She placed one next to the front door of each cottage. In a vacation rental that has a pool or is near a beach, you'll need to help your guests manage wet messes. Install hooks with a sign that reads, ALL WET TOWELS GO ON A HOOK, NOT ON A BED. If your rental features a wood-

Add some special touches that make your guests feel at home. Books, games, wood for the fireplace (if you have one), throws, pillows, mugs, coffee, tea . . . you get the idea. When styling your photo shot make sure to show what a guest might be doing in the space. Here we set up a Scrabble game, some mugs, and pillows to create a cozy, inviting feel.

burning stove or fireplace, you'll have to help your guests use it. Place a sign near the wood for the stove or fireplace that gives step-by-step instructions on how to open the flue, light the kindling, shut the door, and so on. Get creative and have fun with it. We have made playful signs with ripped-out letters from magazine pages (that look like an old detective movie ransom note) for hanging towels, we have created floor mats that have wording across them, and more. Signs can also be used to point out special features of your rental while they tell guests how to use them. A take-and-leave bookshelf, for example, might have a sign that reads, TAKE ONE, LEAVE ONE and also mention that the other books in the rental are personal property (meaning they're not up for grabs).

Think about what might help your guests. Do you have old plumbing that you need to be careful with? Do you want everyone to take off their shoes? Is there a funky step up in a room that you need to point out? Do you want people to smoke on the porch or do you have a specific spot in mind? Do you want to make sure all the windows are closed and locked before folks leave? Don't worry if you forget something—you will find out very quickly what other signage you may need to add, once you start seeing the same issues come up again and again. After doing all this work to create a beautiful design for your space, avoid just writing demands on index cards (such as, "Don't flush anything but TP down the toilet!"). Put something nice together—make it fun, clever, and very, very clear!

Clipboard by the Door

At Main + Mountain Bar & Motel vintage clipboards hang by the door of each room. The clipboard features a piece of brown cardstock. Printed on it is emergency contact info, the Wi-Fi details, and the time when the bar opens . . . all the essentials. This quick access info really spells out the important stuff. And it can come in handier than you might imagine in ways you can't imagine. Put yourself in the place of your guests: what information would you need? Once on vacation in the Caribbean, for example, Joanne was bitten by a scorpion in the house we rented. Sean (the emergency contact) was just down the road bartending, and he rushed up to help. Thankfully, all Joanne needed was a Painkiller (yes, the drink, not the meds). As this little story illustrates, providing emergency contact info and making it easy to find is key to ensuring the well-being of your guests.

A Checklist for When They Leave

Put out a separate sheet (or signage) with a checklist that helps your guests at check out. This checklist should ask questions like: Are the windows closed? Is the heat at _____? Are the blinds shut? Have you checked under the bed for escapee socks? Do you have your phone cord? (Everyone has forgotten one of these.) Do you have all your children? Your wallet? Your backpack? Your toiletries?

Furthermore, this checklist should help your guests help you after they depart. Do they know how to follow you on your Instagram and Facebook accounts? Do they need to leave the key (if so, where)? Whatever is pertinent to your property, make sure it is on the checklist. Make it fun! Make it easy!

Personalization

If you operate an inn, a boutique motel, or a B&B, then you are obviously already personalizing the experience, because you or your staff will be there in person so that someone can be immediately available to your guests. If you are renting your own house or apartment, then you have to work a little harder to ensure that your guests feel welcome, while simultaneously educating them about the rules during their stay in your home. For example, you could put a beautiful basket of new slippers by the door with a framed sign that reads, THANK YOU SO MUCH FOR NOT WEARING YOUR SHOES INDOORS, ENJOY THE SLIPPERS. A presentation like this makes it quite clear that you want folks to take their shoes off at the door. Furthermore, you have provided a cozy service (slippers) while gently and kindly asking your guests to respect your space by not dragging their dirty shoes through it.

Whatever the rules or however you express your wishes, ultimately your goal is to show your guests

Simple Ways to Encourage Good Guests

Signage

Humor

Clipboard with essential details

Guest Binder

Door mats

Lined trash can

Hooks

Towels

Personalized amenities (baskets, token gifts, written notes, and so on)

Check-out checklist

Guestbook (where guests can leave a note)

Clear communication

Coasters

Placemats

Basic cleaning supplies

how much you care about your home, while giving them an opportunity to take care of it. Put one photo of your family having fun in a given area (not shelves full of photographs) such that there's a little touch of personalization. The idea is to help your guests feel a connection with you as well as understand this is your home, not just an impersonal vacation spot. There are many ways you can add personalization to help create good guests—you can use signage, fun photos, or extra amenities that guests don't expect but feel grateful to have. In addition, you can put out a guestbook where guests can leave a note of appreciation. It's the sort of personalized touch that gives your rental positive vibes. But don't just wait until your guests *arrive* to create good guests. Once they book, why not send a lovely personalized note telling them more about your home and its history, fun facts about the area, and a tiny bit about your family (not much)—just enough to let your future guests know you are a hardworking person (just like them) who is sharing your property.

Don't Waste Time

Don't waste your own time. Just as important, don't waste your guests' time. If you personally check in folks to your rental, then you must be at the property when they arrive. If you promise an item in the house, then it must be there and working properly. Following through on your promises seems like obvious common sense, and it is. But if you don't get the small things right, then you are starting off on the wrong foot with your guests. Remember that your guests are coming to your inn, vacation rental, or boutique motel because they want an authentic experience—something real, something local, and maybe something a little bit adventurous . . . but that adventure doesn't extend to no-show hosts, island-time check ins, or bathrooms with no toilet paper (yes, it happens). You must provide the basic services and amenities guests would expect and receive at a conventional hotel. The more you plan ahead and the better you manage your operation, the more likely it is your guests will experience a smooth stay and the more likely you are to have good guests. So as not to waste anyone's time, you must effectively run your check-in process, provide a great Guest Binder (provide online once a guest books with you and put it at the rental), keep your amenities fully stocked and up to date, and make sure all the other details are up to snuff.

A Complete Guest Binder

Another way to make life easier for your guests (and in turn, you) is to create a very detailed Guest Binder. It can be pretty, informative, and clever. You should know that there are three types of guests: those who prefer to get their information online, those who enjoy looking through a physical binder, and those who like both. So to please everyone (well, as many people as you can, because we all know you can't please everyone), create a digital binder that can be accessed online as well as a physical binder that's located in your rental. In addition to this book, some great suggestions for your Guest Binder can be found online at Vacation Rental Formula (www.vacationrentalformula.com). Topics should range from how to get into the building; where to park; how to use the fireplace, stove, TV, thermostat, and so on; suggestions on where to eat; how to check out; and of course, emergency contact information. The Guest Binder at the rental itself can also contain city maps and trail maps, menus, and a guest comment section. Have some fun with it!

Guest Binder Suggestions

Welcome letter (thanking guests for visiting)

Emergency contact information page

Table of contents (what is in the Guest Binder)

House rules (shoes off at the door, noise, and other important rules)

What to do upon arrival (where to park, turning on the heat, and so forth)

What to do upon departure (turning down the heat, making sure the windows are closed, and so on)

How to use the fireplace, stove, TV, thermostat, and the rest

Manuals that go with each piece of tech or appliance (if you have them)

Directions to popular attractions

List of favorite restaurants

Suggestions for what to do in the area

List of favorite hiking trails (or popular recreation activities in your area)

Specifics that relate to your property (using the pool, the gas grill, and the like)

Specifics that relate to your location (ski areas, beaches, lakes, and so forth)

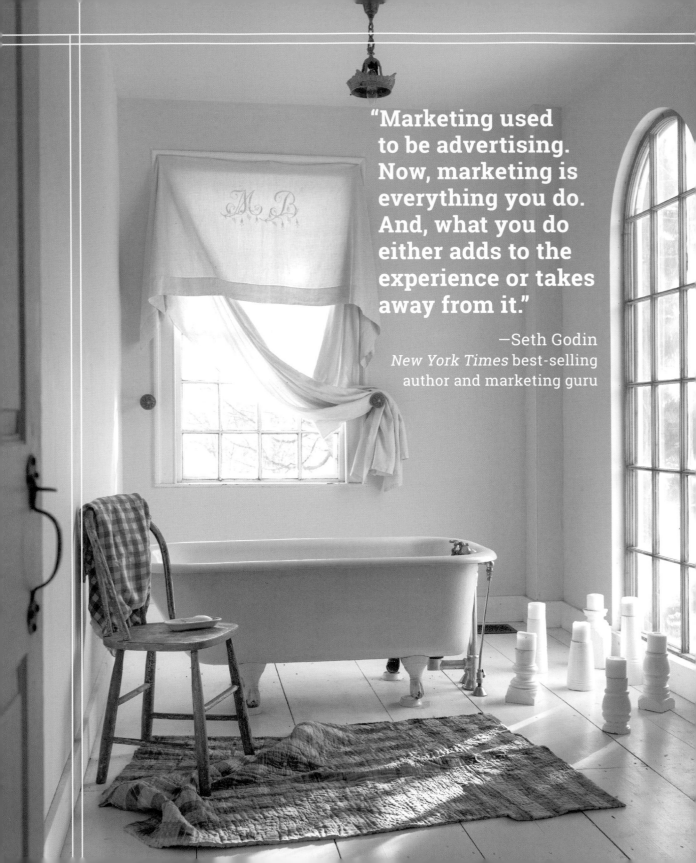

"Marketing used to be advertising. Now, marketing is everything you do. And, what you do either adds to the experience or takes away from it."

—Seth Godin
New York Times best-selling author and marketing guru

Chapter ❸
Design Is Marketing

In today's world of vacation rentals and boutique hospitality, design *is* marketing. This is not your traditional "build your marketing plan" chapter. Instead it covers the important design details that are at play in your marketing. As you undoubtedly know already, customers' expectations in vacation rentals and boutique hospitality have only increased over the past years. This means that showing off your property's unique personality is important for differentiating yourself in this competitive market. So when we say that "a picture is worth a thousand words," we really mean it. Guests today are looking for "experience travel," which means your design has to tell a story.

In this chapter, we outline some marketing basics and budget-friendly ideas that will help you show off your designs and connect with your target audience. If you really want to get after your marketing and you have some additional funds, then you can hire some professional help in an effort to boost your bookings and profits. We know some brilliant folks and products that work specifically on vacation rental marketing, and you'll find them listed in Chapter 4.

Great photography is key to the success of your rental. Without great photographs, your marketing efforts will be much more difficult to pull off or even impossible to accomplish. Wendy Lewis of Textile Trunk let us style her beautiful bathroom with her vintage pieces. This shows just how important great photography and amazing styling are to marketing your rental.

Facts and Stories

According to some statistics from Airbnb, quality photography will pay for itself with a 40-percent increase in earnings, 24 percent more bookings, and 25 percent higher nightly prices. Matt Landau at VRMB (www.vrmb .com), did a quick experiment using his own photos versus hiring a photographer. The results weren't even close. The professional photos increased his profits by more than five times! Hire a professional.

Homework: List the marketing tactics you are already doing today. After you read through the next few marketing ideas and suggestions, go back to your list to see which ones you can improve upon, which ones you should stop doing, and which ones you need to implement. Don't forget to always have your Audience Profiles on hand (see page 22). Use these profiles to make sure your marketing channels align with where your customers are getting their information about your rental.

From a marketing tactics standpoint we recommend at minimum you should have:

• Great photography (and video)

• Strong listing on booking platforms

• Your own website

• Social media

• Customer communication

• Encouragement of 5-star reviews

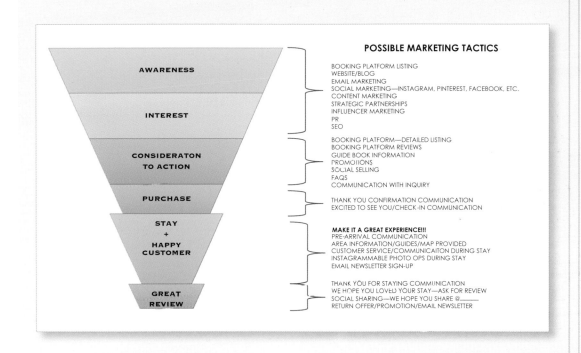

POSSIBLE MARKETING TACTICS

AWARENESS

INTEREST

BOOKING PLATFORM LISTING
WEBSITE/BLOG
EMAIL MARKETING
SOCIAL MARKETING—INSTAGRAM, PINTEREST, FACEBOOK, ETC.
CONTENT MARKETING
STRATEGIC PARTNERSHIPS
INFLUENCER MARKETING
PR
SEO

CONSIDERATON TO ACTION

BOOKING PLATFORM—DETAILED LISTING
BOOKING PLATFORM REVIEWS
GUIDE BOOK INFORMATION
PROMOTIONS
SOCIAL SELLING
FAQS
COMMUNICATION WITH INQUIRY

PURCHASE

THANK YOU CONFIRMATION COMMUNICATION
EXCITED TO SEE YOU/CHECK-IN COMMUNICATION

STAY
+
HAPPY CUSTOMER

MAKE IT A GREAT EXPERIENCE!!!
PRE-ARRIVAL COMMUNICATION
AREA INFORMATION/GUIDES/MAP PROVIDED
CUSTOMER SERVICE/COMMUNICAITON DURING STAY
INSTAGRAMMABLE PHOTO OPS DURING STAY
EMAIL NEWSLETTER SIGN-UP

GREAT REVIEW

THANK YOU FOR STAYING COMMUNICATION
WE HOPE YOU LOVED YOUR STAY—ASK FOR REVIEW
SOCIAL SHARING—WE HOPE YOU SHARE @_____
RETURN OFFER/PROMOTION/EMAIL NEWSLETTER

MARKETING WHAT? MARKETING FUNNEL

Let's start in the clouds—high-level stuff, as Rosanne calls it. Rosanne likes to start with a Marketing Funnel (basically following a customer's journey from start to finish) that highlights some possible marketing tactics specific to this industry. Joanne prefers to go straight into the styling. In this case, Rosanne won. Joanne had to get her to promise not to build a Decision-Making Tree. It's the small wins that count.

We go back and forth about showing people in photos that market rental properties. Trends are always changing and you'll find listings with architectural photos, lifestyle photos, and influencers' photos (more on that on page 161). We recommend that you do not put people in your general photos—the pages (galleries) you use to show off your property and rooms. Your guests want to imagine themselves sitting around that table, not your cute brother (unless he comes with the place). That said, if you want to add some people shots for your social media, blog, or other review pages, go for it. It may be fun. We love the website of the Stay Lokal (staylokal.com). Their listing profiles both the rooms (no people) and the social scene (with people).

Show Off! Styling and Photography

One of the most important aspects of getting bookings is the photography and styling of your place. Incredibly, it is often overlooked. Visuals are critical in our visual world, and the ever-growing competition in the boutique hospitality and vacation rental market means that you must put your best "photography" foot forward.

Good photography and how to use it in your marketing (booking platforms, website, print materials, and social media) are key to your success. There are no ifs, ands, or buts about it. Don't be shy! That's right, get out there and strut your stuff. Styling your spaces to make them look stunning and realistic gives you an edge on your competitors and will be appreciated by your (potential) guests.

Photography and styling, if done correctly, will transform your spaces and your rental rates—just be sure not to over promise in your photography and under deliver in reality. Your hosting platform will give you tons of tips on how to take your own great photos, and they will provide guidelines on how to prepare your space for a professional photographer. We adamantly recommend that you hire a professional if you can afford it.

If, for whatever reason, you don't have access to professional photography, then at least get the basics down in the photos you take yourself. You'd be surprised how often the first shot of a bathroom shows the toilet seat up and messy towels hanging, or a bedroom features an unmade bed. How is anyone going to trust a host who can't even manage to make the bed for the photo? Your photography is not just about beautiful photos, it is about building trust, creating experiences, and showing off your personality.

Your marketing images should be a mix of inside shots, detail shots, lifestyle shots, outside shots, neighborhood shots, and local and regional photos. Let's first consider inside, detail, and lifestyle shots. We'll then work our way outside.

This is a detail shot of the gathering room at Bear Mountain Inn after the renovations. We could have just taken the shot with the custom ottoman and chairs, and it would have been pretty. But why not go the extra mile and create a beautiful lifestyle image? We added the beer, snacks, playing cards, blanket, and vintage game on the extra-large ottoman. Not only do prospective guests get to see what the space looks like, but they get to imagine themselves sitting in it while enjoying a beer with a friend and playing a game. Style your shots with realistic items and materials that are either at the location or are available to your guests.

Before

This is an iPhone shot of a bedroom in Sonoma, California. It's a nice room that features good bedding and a good use of space, but does this shot wow you? Think about easy, affordable ways to enhance this space to make the image more impressive.

After

Here is the same Sonomoa bedroom at a slightly different camera angle, after a five-minute styling using some extra pillows, a lumbar pillow for a pop of color, some flowers in a vase, and a throw blanket. This is also a good time to find out what type of photos you are looking for, be it mostly vertical, horizontal, or square. Think about how the images appear on the booking platform as well as your marketing needs. When planning your photo shoot, schedule it for the time of day when the natural light in the room is at its best.

What sort of photos should you post if you only have one or two rooms available to rent? Of course, you will want to include overall room shots to give potential guests an architectural understanding of the space. But you should also add photos that will give your potential guests an emotional feel for your space, plus some close-up detail shots that allow guests to picture themselves in the space. The emphasis is on the experience of staying in the rental. The Holly Vault Crossing House, a Victorian inn-turned-Airbnb in Holly, Michigan, pays homage to its Victorian roots with select vintage pieces and pops of color that are designed to catch the eye of potential guests as they scroll through listings for a place to stay.

Before

DESIGN THOUGHT PROCESS: TURNING OUTDATED TO OUTSTANDING

Joanne had a blast with this project. She worked with the owners on the interior design goal of keeping the character of this historic barn, while modernizing it into an eco-friendly vacation home. After all the old furniture was removed (it was donated to local organizations), the character of the space was revealed. Modern windows were installed and the walls were painted white, which allowed the character of the post-and-beam architecture to shine through.

After the project was completed, a professional photographer was hired to document the space. Joanne, the architect, and the project manager shared this cost. Joanne styled the spaces for the photos, which is typically an undervalued aspect of preparation. She considered everything from the angle of the chairs to the vase on the table to how the dishes were displayed. Even though these styling touches are lovely, they don't take away from what the shot is all about—the architecture itself and the view. Take a moment to review how some of your favorite spaces, hospitality locations, and vacation rentals are styled. This will help you get a sense of how you might style photographs that will appeal to your target market.

After

Joanne has a thing for turning closets into something else. This oversized closet now houses bunk beds in this Stowe, Vermont, rental. The overall room shot shows another twin bed and a dresser, but this detail shot is all about the bunks. Styled with kids' books, a truck, other toys, extra pillows, and a throw blanket, it looks lived in and inviting. Showing the corner of the skylight puts the detail shot in perspective, which helps potential guests imagine its location in the room.

After Joanne finishes her design projects, she often styles them for photographs. This renovated kitchen was styled to show off its modern farmhouse feel. Joanne brought in some glass jars for cereals, a wooden bowl for apples, a cutting board, coffee, and plants in modern containers. Mixing and matching old and new, and adding plant life and food, brought life to this beautiful space. We cannot express how important your photography will be on your booking platform, your marketing efforts, and your return on investment. Just remember, if you take away all the details in your photography and your guests show up to an empty kitchen that only has a couple of plates, they will be sorely disappointed. It's okay to add a little bit of greenery, flowers, food, and a pillow or two for the photo shoot. But for major décor pieces, only style with items that guests will realistically expect to find in place when they arrive.

The emphasis of this close-up photograph is the beautiful custom-made wool blanket. Notice that the background is faded out. This style of photography is a great way to suggest a feeling. Here, the feeling is of comfort and warmth. This renovation project, which produced detail-worthy motel rooms, was designed by TruexCullins Architecture and Interior Design. Joanne was part of the design team.

Don't Forget Video

When you're thinking about photography to highlight your property, don't forget about animations and video. In addition to YouTube and Instagram, you can post video on your website. The video options are endless—using a drone, you can shoot video of just about anything outside your property and your surroundings.

For example, the website for Cliff House in Cape Neddick, Maine, has a terrific video on its home page (www.cliffhousemaine.com). Granted, this is a gorgeous, luxury hotel with a large marketing budget; that shouldn't stop you from seeing what great online marketing can look like. If you visit the site, you'll notice that the images at the top of the home page do not show any of their rooms. This marketing is all about selling an experience (not a room). Your marketing should be about that, too. With a little reflection, you'll probably come up with dozens of ideas. Maybe you'll highlight the food you serve with a short (five second) clip, or maybe you'll emphasize the ocean view in front of the property with a slow panning shot, or maybe you'll use hiking videos to show the adventures that can be had on the mountain trails behind your property. Start small and put together experience pieces that your guests will want to be a part of. The same holds true for a professional videographer as it does a photographer: If you can, hire a professional. A budget-friendly option is to hire high school and college students who are in video workshops or who are majoring in video production. This kind of work builds their résumé, they work at reasonable rates, and the results are often outstanding. Don't forget that booking platforms have tons of resources as well.

Facts and Stories

There is a new type of marketing out there called "influencers." Basically, these are individuals (or couples or a group) who market brands by taking photos of themselves using a product or being at a location and then showing those photos to their followers. It is the wild, wild West out there in the world of influencers, and before you swing open your saloon doors to just anyone you should really understand how this type of branding and marketing works. *The Atlantic* magazine published a great article about it called, "Instagram's Wannabe-Stars Are Driving Luxury Hotels Crazy." Read it to learn how this form of marketing works and doesn't work. But this is just one source. Read up on the subject to determine if this type of marketing could benefit you. It might not. Regardless, you should at least have a plan in place for when you will (or will not) include an influencer in your marketing strategy.

Before

DESIGN THOUGHT PROCESS: SHOWING OFF THE MORE USEABLE SPACE

This after photo was taken in the doorway of the first room. It shows how the rooms connect, which is a great way for potential guests to get a feel for the space. At Bear Mountain Inn, located in Waterford, Maine, Joanne worked with owners Julie and Brian Sullivan to figure out how guests were actually using the rooms at the inn and how the rooms could be better utilized. This particular room didn't really feel comfortable before the renovation. The bed was too close to both the window and doorway, and the twin beds located in the other room of the suite competed with the oversized closet. You could do nothing but sleep in the room. We placed the bed on the wall opposite the windows, created a built-in bunk for the smaller room, and removed the closet. This gave us room to place a television, a table, and some chairs in the suite.

The resulting rooms were more inviting and usable. The barn door slider helped us save space (without the swing of a door, there is more usable square feet) and added character to the room. The décor is simple here—a plant on a stand, a throw pillow, a vintage barn door hinge in a shadow box, and a plaid blanket to play off the plaid wallpaper. You can see how the photography captures the new flow, and how this renovation has completely transformed these two rooms.

After

We are big fans of detailed artistic shots like this. Notice how the natural light flows into the kitchen and bounces off the bowls and spoons. A marketing caption for this photograph could be something like, "Our well-equipped kitchen is filled with light and plenty of wooden spoons for the chef in the family." Use natural light whenever possible in your photography. Moreover, whether you are taking photos yourself or getting ready for a professional to come, you must make sure the space is very clean and presentable. In bedrooms, the sheets and pillowcases must be ironed and looking crisp, and the bedding must be straightened out and put together; in bathrooms, the toilet seat should be down, the towels folded neatly, the toiletries filled and straightened up, and all clutter eliminated.

The Importance of Branding

Rosanne once heard a marketing expert describe to a client the difference between brand and marketing: "A brand is like designing and building a beautiful car, but it just sits in the driveway without marketing. Good marketing drives it around the right neighborhoods so everyone can see it, desire it, and want to own it."

We understand that branding is not always that simple, but for this chapter we are going to oversimplify to highlight the importance of doing at least the minimum for your property. Our motto is also simple: Do less, better.

Vacation rentals and boutique properties with character are the norm in today's hospitality industry. Competition is fierce in most markets, and your guests will have enough experience to expect (and demand) more than what used to be acceptable. It is no longer good enough to just have clean sheets and an ordinary space. To stand out among the competition you must differentiate yourself. Creating a strong brand personality that excites and inspires your guests is what puts you ahead of the competition—and is what causes them to select your listing.

Build Your Brand Kit

- Brand logo

- Your personality/voice (are you down to earth, sophisticated, quirky, rugged?)

- Brand font

- Brand colors

- Brand mission (why you exist)

- Listing descriptor (name of your rental and a quick description)

- Brand keywords (keywords you use in your marketing and social media)

- Photography and video guidelines

- Design and styling guidelines

- Other areas specific to you and your property

Brand Homework:

- Do all your marketing elements tell the same brand story?

- Does it all look like it belongs together?

- Do all your furnishings, fixtures, styling, special touches, and signage align with your font and logo style, marketing copy, messaging, descriptions, and photography?

- Does it align with the title of your listing, web address, website, social media contact info, and so forth?

- Do you feel the whole thing comes together? (For example, does your mid-century furniture match the fonts on your marketing materials and your descriptions? Does your Mission-style home feel consistent with the photography filters you've used and your branding?)

- Do you have all the important elements of your Brand Kit covered?

- Do you have all your creative and branding materials stored in one location?

- Are your digital brand materials backed up locally (flash drives, a second computer) or at a cloud-storage location?

- Are your brand materials both secure and easily accessible? You should never have to re-create anything, nor should you miss out on marketing opportunities because you can't find something.

As we already mentioned, photography is probably one (if not the) most important way to visually create your brand. A picture really is worth a thousand words, and designing with photography in mind is critical. But there are a few more elements you need to consider when developing your brand.

Your brand represents who you are (or what your space is), and personalizing your brand helps you stand out from the crowd. Brand personalization is expressed in everything you do, from the imagery on your website and Instagram to the signage in your property. It helps you authentically engage with your audience. We talked a bit about the importance of knowing yourself and your audience in the beginning of the book. This knowledge is critical not only to finding your tribe but to building your brand and to personalizing it so as to engage them.

Be consistent. Consistent messaging, imagery, and voice will not only better resonate with your audience, but it will establish trust and will help you build your brand faster. To help with consistency you should have a Brand Kit that you or your team can always refer to. Your Brand Kit should contain a few essentials.

As homework, try to build your Brand Kit. Clear off the dining room table and put out whatever you have from the checklist onto the table: logos, photos, marketing copy, social media posts, Facebook pages, Airbnb listings, photos of your rental, and so on. Look at it all very carefully. Be objective. Compare it against the lists in this book. Get unbiased feedback from people you trust. Have friends look at it.

While doing this homework, remember you can't be everything to everyone. You must find your uniqueness. This will help you find your focus. If you need more help building your brand, look in Chapter 4 for several great suggestions.

Here, Joanne is putting up the last details of the renovation at Main + Mountain Bar & Motel in Ludlow, Vermont. Two years before Joanne was working out the designs for this room, she met an artist from Citizen Woodshop at a *Country Living* magazine fair. She got his card. She remembered him while working on this renovation, and she called him up and asked him to make these custom wooden Vermont maps. They are unique, relevant to the project, and support an artist. If you see something you love, get the maker's card and put it in your dream file. You never know when you may give them a call. The vintage clipboard now hangs next to the entrance light in the bedroom. It features a page with emergency contact information and other important facts—including the bar hours—using the motel's branded font, typeface, and logo. When you do your renovation, make sure you set aside some funds for these kinds of detail pieces.

The Importance of Keywords

SEO? SEM? Did you pick up the wrong type of book? No, let us explain.

SEO stands for search engine optimization, and SEM stands for search engine marketing. The basic difference is that SEO efforts help deliver better "organic" search results, whereas SEM is a "paid" search effort that aims to drive more traffic to a website or listing. Basically, everyone wants to be on the first page of a search, be it on Google or a hosting platform such as Airbnb. This is extremely difficult to achieve, but that's where SEO and SEM helps.

Caveat here. To explain all that is involved with SEO and SEM would require another book. Needless to say, you can and should spend some serious time learning about this (see Chapter 4 for suggested resources). You can hire out SEO and SEM activities to professional marketers. This isn't a bad idea, especially because this is a moving target—search engine algorithms change often.

That being said, search engine algorithms thrive on data. This means that the more "relevant" information you can provide, the better your results. Keywords are the words that your audience may use in a search to find a property like yours. By having these keywords in your listing and online content, you help search engines find you. This, in turn, increases your visibility.

Remember that Audience Profile we had you do at the beginning of the book? Use that to help you develop a list of keywords that are relevant to your audience. This master list will be your reference guide as you develop your marketing, which includes your listing profile, social media efforts, and website content. When naming your listing or creating your domain name (website URL), use keywords when possible. This will help with SEO. If your rental is a houseboat in the Seattle area, for example, your listing and domain might be: Seattle Houseboat Vacation Rental, www.SeattleHouseboatVacationRental.com.

Hosting platforms such as Airbnb, HomeAway, VRBO, and the like all have great resources on how to improve SEO through listing descriptions on their platform. We highly suggest you take the time to read these resources and to do the work to improve your listing descriptors for better results.

As the Seattle houseboat example illustrates, the actual title of your rental should contain keywords. Your rental may be called Bob's House, but really, how the heck is that going to help you when folks are searching for "cottages by the sea"? No one, and we mean no one, will search for "Bob's House." A better title for SEO would be "Oceanfront Cottage on Barefoot Beach" or "Cottage on Florida's Barefoot Beach." This would certainly find its way to a potential guest faster. In your description feel free to use the name of the rental, but load it up with keywords: "At Bob's House, an oceanfront one-bedroom cottage located directly on Barefoot Beach, you can enjoy the sound of the waves from your private front porch. Walk out your door and be on Barefoot Beach, voted the best beach on the Gulf Coast in Naples, Florida. This beach is known for its white sand, warm water, and dolphin sightings." Notice how cleverly we were able to add a bunch of keywords in these few sentences.

Again, go back to your handy Audience Profile and see what your guests care about. What are they searching for? What are some of the specific words they might use? Design style? Destination? Location? Type of home? Number of bedrooms? Amenities? What are the relevant local attractions? Is it a sporting event, a conference center, a music hall, something else? The more specific you can get the better. Whether it's unique design, special amenities, cool neighborhood, landmarks, city or state college . . . make sure each term you use is a keyword. We mean, if you're renting out your cool mid-century house in Palm Springs, California, once owned by Frank Sinatra, then by all means, shout that out. If you've got it, flaunt it.

Do not over promise and under deliver with your keywords or descriptions. Keep guest expectations realistic when you create your listing. "Next to beach" is very different from "One mile away from beach"; "Eight blocks from Nashville's music scene" is very different from "In the heart of Nashville's music scene"; "Right out the door is the best hiking along the Path of the Gods on the Amalfi Coast in Italy" is different from "Close to the best hiking on the Amalfi Coast." The more landmarks, towns, restaurants, hikes, mud wrestling tournaments, or whatever you can list in your descriptions, the more words you will have for broad and narrow searches. But . . . and this is the *big* but . . . because it will come to bite you in the rear if you don't do this . . . *be very clear* how close or far you are to something. Be honest about what you can offer and where your rental is located.

Joanne once searched high and low for the perfect boutique lodging in Greece (outside of Athens near the coast). She fell in love with the photos of a boutique resort that had a farm, a donkey, and gorgeous outside restaurant seating. She booked it for two nights and traveled there with her daughter and husband. Upon arrival they discovered that "the farm and its restaurant" were about a 10-minute car ride away, and were only open on Thursday, Friday, and Saturday nights (they were visiting on Sunday and Monday; go figure). Talk about disappointed. Nowhere on the listing did it say, "The farm and restaurant are miles from where you sleep and are not always open."

We feel very strongly about not over promising, be it through text or photographs. The photos you post should make it very clear where your rental is and how far it is from the other locations you mention. If you say the rental is near the beach, potential guests might rightly think they can grab a beach chair out of the garage and walk a few minutes to the beach. But if in reality your guests have to get in the car and drive 10 minutes to get to the beach, you will have disappointed guests who might write a bad review: "We were not even close to the beach! We had to drive 10 minutes, total pain in the butt." But if you properly set expectations, those same guests might leave a review like this: "We loved our stay. They had a handy beach kit with an umbrella, chairs, towels, and sunscreen that we just threw in the trunk of our car. What a great beach. We will be back."

Using keywords as you describe your design style and amenities can drastically help with SEO. We can't tell you how many times "boho style" gets searched by millennial women, or how many times the term "farmhouse style" is used by folks who want to visit wine country.

What are the terms people would use for your area? Think about what people might be searching for in a rental: lots of bedrooms, a pool, a gourmet kitchen, air-conditioning, hiking, biking, farmhouses, an island retreat. Make sure you describe what you have to offer, but do so honestly. If your rental has three bedrooms with a double bed, a queen bed, and a king bed, then you can honestly say that the rental sleeps six. If your rental has a tiny couch with a pull-out mattress for its sleeping accommodation, think twice before saying the rental can sleep eight.

As for the description itself, we suggest you paint a picture. You have spent so much energy on creating a uniquely designed space. Describe it. "You will sleep soundly in this master bedroom. A modern oasis with its warm white walls, luxurious Ralph Lauren leather headboard, Sleep Number mattress with super soft organic cotton sheets, plush down comforter, and faux fur throw blanket."

With amenities, don't assume folks will know what you have. You may have a coffeepot but not coffee, you may have a toaster but not a microwave. List all the amenities you do have—especially if you think they will really appeal to your guests for your specific area. Have a place in Sonoma, California? Then list the use of two beach cruiser bicycles, picnic basket and blankets, and wine carrier . . . wonderful things for a couple who wants to go into town, sit on the green, watch a band play, and drink some wine. You can appeal to professionals and techies with high-speed Internet, a desk area, Apple TV, a Nest video doorbell, secure Wi-Fi, touch key locks, and so forth.

It all comes back to knowing your audience and which features your rental has to make your place attractive to them. Be sure to work with your hosting platform to explore more ways to improve your SEO, such as customer-service offerings, host information, and the like. Don't forget to use close-up lifestyle shots of some of your best amenities. *And* use your social media for SEO. Choosing the keywords to #hashtag helps improve your visibility online.

Joanne made this custom word search for a pizza restaurant called Pizza 44 in Burlington, Vermont. The photographer herself got in the shot to show it being used. This gives life to the picture, which is important when you're shooting something interactive—say a beach, boat, diving board, games, or a pub. That said, be judicious when putting people in your photos. The majority of your photos should not feature people. If you do feature people, you can blur them like in this shot. Or you can have their faces turned away, or you can use a group shot of people laughing, cooking, reading— acting natural, not posing.

Possible Blog Post Ideas

New and exciting design features at _____ (your property)

Drinks and music in old town _____

Our favorite hangouts on _____ Street

Things to do on a Sunday in _____

Breakfast—my favorite meal of the day

Did someone say pizza and beer?

Local wine bars I love _____, _____, and _____

If I only had 24 hours in _____

Date night in _____

Mixology experts describe the best cocktails in _____

Three nights, four days for the adventure traveler

Three nights, four days for the romantic

Three nights, four days for the beer lover

Sleep in, what we offer for fun

Our 10 favorite places to eat

Our 10 favorite places to hike

Sharing our most popular recipe for chocolate chip cookies

Our favorite artists

Our 10 favorite events in _____ (town)

Our favorite art festivals in _____ (city)

Our 10 favorite _____ (state) events

Six almost-secret bicycle loops

Antiques and salvage shopping near us

The local products and artisans we use in our inn

Our favorite drives in the fall

Fall foliage tours

Romantic things to do in _____

The best books to curl up with on a rainy day

Our beach toys

Your Website and Hosting Platforms

In this section, we won't show you how to build your own website or to create the perfect listing on a hosting platform. But we will remind you that first impressions matter. And they matter just as much online as they do in person. Make sure your first encounter with your audience is designed to invite a stay. It bears repeating: Whether your customer discovers your property on a booking platform like VRBO, Airbnb, your own website, or your Instagram post, your brand personality should shine through and be consistent at every touch point.

Even if you only book your property via hosting platforms, we highly recommend you have your own website. Why, you ask? Your own website:

- Allows you to show off your own unique design, highlight the personality of your property, and build your brand
- Enables you to share much more information than what appears on a listing platform
- Is controlled by you and not the rules of the listing site
- Facilitates guests to search for your property directly and possibly to book directly, too
- Can feature your social media sites, such as Instagram
- Allows you to build your own database and community
- Helps you to market directly to your database via e-newsletters, email promotions, and the like
- Can host a blog and updatable content for improved SEO
- Helps you build trust

If you already have a website, *great!* Now, we ask that you grab a cup of coffee (Rosanne suggests wine) and review your website page by page, objectively. Does it match the brand personality and design style you have created?

If you don't have a website, get building one. You can build one yourself (platforms like WordPress, Wix, and Squarespace make this easy to do). There are also many resources that specialize in creating websites for vacation rentals. We list a few in Chapter 4. Your website does not have to be huge. You can start with just a few pages and build from there. But those few pages should be designed to excite viewers and to entice people to stay and find out more.

Facts and Stories

Don't let marketing go on the back burner (like our exercise programs always seem to do). It deserves allocated time, whether it is 30 minutes a day or a few hours a week, or more. Regardless, it needs to happen regularly and consistently. If you're overwhelmed in terms of time and don't have a large budget, hire a college intern to help. Marketing majors who specialize in social media and branding can be of great help. They can work with you to put together a plan and help you execute it. We have worked with interns for many years and have had great success. We even had an entire public relations class take on a specific project for us. It was great fun, and the students earned real life experience that was tangible and relatable to their studies.

Before

DESIGN THOUGHT PROCESS: GET A NEW COUCH AND GET IT OFF THE WALL

There are times when you just have to say, "We need a new couch." Look at what your guests are saying in their reviews and private messages to you. If they are commenting about your furnishings or saying your place feels outdated, then you need to think about refreshing things. Also pay attention to which photos people are looking at and how many bookings you received, and then do the math. Would updating the space and uploading new photos help boost your bookings? If the answer is yes—which it was here—then see if getting something new will help boost your number of stays.

Here, it was all about getting a new couch and getting it away from the wall. It's easy to push a couch against a wall, but most of the time it looks much better if it's placed farther out in the room. In this vacation rental townhouse, Joanne purchased new furniture and placed a sofa table behind the couch. Since there weren't any reading lights in the room, this was a great place to add lighting. This lighting can be used for reading and relaxing, and it can be turned off when the televsion is on. The "new" coffee table used to be a dining table; Joanne cut the legs down and added a metal top. The poufs add extra seating without taking up too much space in the room. They can easily be pushed under the coffee table to get them out of the way. She grabbed a bunch of baskets at a secondhand shop, painted a few, and used them on the wall to create very affordable décor. Whenever Joanne uses curtains, she tries to add sheers. These allow guests to choose the amount of privacy they would like.

As an added bonus, all the old furniture that was in the house was donated to the local Habitat for Humanity store (yes, even that couch). With the new furniture added, the room styled and professionally photographed, and the images posted on the property's website, hosting sites, and social media outlets, the bookings skyrocketed.

After

No matter what size your website is, you should start collecting names from day one. You can have a simple offer that is exciting enough that people will give you their email address. Building your database is critical for future marketing efforts, such as e-newsletters or emails. You can get creative in your communications. Examples include Happy Birthday wishes, special promotions, event information, and updates on your rental. Developing a communications calendar is an ideal way to help you develop relevant content for your community. It also helps to make sure you do not overuse your list.

We like blogs, but we are guilty of not having the time to keep one going consistently. If you have the time, we highly recommend that you keep a blog on your website. It is a great way to keep content fresh and helps with SEO. Maintaining a blog does not have to be overwhelming. It could be as simple as a monthly post where you write about a local place, nearby adventures, local events, or even a three-day weekend getaway idea. Not only will you be promoting your community and all the amazing businesses in it, but you will be giving free and helpful advice, which folks greatly appreciate. As a result, these folks will be more likely to consider you as a location to stay, versus someone who doesn't communicate with them.

We don't need to tell you how important your booking (hosting) platform listing is. But we do want to remind you that these hosting platforms *want* you to succeed; if you win, they win. They have the best resources on how to improve your listing using their service. Read them. We don't even come close to having the experience and advice they offer.

What we *can* offer you is advice about presentation. You should absolutely use your new and improved design features and brand personality in your listing description to help you stand out in the crowd. This is where you can paint a picture with words, and add keywords whenever possible. For example, don't say: "Two bikes included." Do say: "Cruise around Sonoma's historic square, local wineries, and vineyards with our two complimentary bikes with baskets to carry your picnic basket and wine glasses." Revisit the SEO section in this chapter for more information about painting a picture while using keywords when writing or editing your listing.

Large hosting platforms such as Airbnb, VRBO, and HomeAway also provide property owners with marketing opportunities. Their e-newsletters, magazines, social media, or other outlets can be a huge opportunity for you to get millions of eyeballs on your vacation rental, so make sure you are aware of these opportunities. At the very least, make sure you receive their e-newsletters so you can see what the competition is up to.

If It's Not on Instagram . . . Did It Really Happen?

Instagram, Facebook, Pinterest, Twitter . . . oh my! People started using social media to catch up with friends and family, and it has now become one of the most widely used communication channels in the world. People use it for many facets of their life, from connecting with friends to searching for their next vacation to business advice to shopping. This is our new world. You can try to deny it or ignore it, but do so at your own peril. If you haven't yet embraced social media, get started today.

You can certainly place all your information on your booking platform, have your great pics there, and call it a day. Let the rest happen on its own. But, if you really want to increase your exposure, your bookings, and your branding, then we highly recommend you create and post on the social media channels that are important to your target audience. The good news is you don't have to do them all; you just need to choose one or two and do them well. Look at Instagram, Pinterest, Facebook, and the rest as opportunities where you get to show off your property, your location, and the benefits to staying in your rental. Don't forget to bring your personality into your stories to make you stand out.

So many vacation rentals do an amazing job getting recognized via Instagram. Check out accounts for Urban Cowboy, Mountain Modern Motel, Main + Mountain Bar & Motel, The Kutcher Condo, Homestyle Hostel, Bunkhouse Group, The Vintage Round Top, Hotel Vermont, The Beach Lodge, Freehand Hotels, Shelter Social Club, Lokal Hotel, The Ramble Hotel, This Old Hudson, The Line Hotels, Hewing Hotel, and The Jennings Hotel, just to name a few. See where your target market is doing their social media and focus on those sites. Remember, on social media, design sells.

Facts and Stories

According to Insights, a reporting service of Pinterest, 40 million plus people in the United States use Pinterest every month for travel ideas. That is a lot of people! Pinterest also has SEO. This means that when you post boards, make sure to use keywords. See Chapter 4 for information about a great podcast that focuses on how to use Pinterest in your marketing efforts.

Homework: Consider How You Can Boost Bookings with Online Branding

Which are the best social media platforms to use to reach your audience?

Which topics are my audience searching for?

List a few ways you can use your design style and brand personality in stories.

What is the best time for me to find 15 minutes a day to update my social media—updating, commenting, and posting?

Who should I follow that is relevant to my target audience?

Who should I follow to get inspired by how they are posting photos of their lodging, location, and beautiful lifestyle shots?

What inspires me about their posts? Which of their posts gets liked or shared the most?

Are they posting about just their rooms or showing lifestyle shots, local things to do, and encouraging interaction?

What clever ways can I share my space? (Don't worry if you have only one room to rent. Some of our favorite sites post the same rooms, over and over again, changing up the topic or changing around a few textiles, décor pieces, and some staging.)

Do I have a space that is Instagrammable? Can I design one?

On this trip to Italy, we stayed in an authentic trullo house in Alberobello, a UNESCO World Heritage Site. It was a tiny cone-shaped house that elves could have lived in. So cool! This bicycle was in the perfect position for a photo op and Rosanne took full advantage. Did this photo hit her social media sites? You bet it did. Clever, meaningful, and authentic décor that allows your guest to shout about you from the rooftops—or at least from their phones—will only help your business.

How can you get started? Encourage your guests to follow you, tag you, and share you. Use smart design to make Instagrammable moments. Also make it even easier for guests by creating locations that they will want to be photographed in.

Don't be afraid to ask your guests to follow you on social media, or to mention and tag you in their shots while they are visiting. Really think through your posts and your hashtags. Mix broad hashtags like, #vermont with narrow hashtags like, #vermontwedding and #vermontcountrywedding. Be thoughtful in your captions and encourage engagement. Remember your goals: to have folks get to know you and your property, like you, and trust you enough to stay at your place. Crediting others is important as well. Don't forget to mention the people and businesses who play a role in your décor and community. First and foremost, it is a nice thing to do, and second it shows you care about supporting these businesses. And if you support them, then maybe, just maybe, they will support you back. If you purchased the lighting from Target, then tag them . . . bedding from Parachute, tag them . . . if you have a favorite pizza joint, tag them . . . a local historical place to visit, yes, you guessed it . . . tag them!

A quick reminder: many social media channels are also searchable, so SEO best practices pertain here as well. Use keywords when posting and with #hashtags and @locations. For example, if your guests are planning to travel to St. Barts, they may search Pinterest by typing in keywords that are relevant to their trip, say: "St. Barts Hiking Trails." Now, imagine a picture comes up with a gorgeous shot of a hiking trail with words across it saying, "The Top Best 5 Hiking Trails on St. Barts, by Serene Beach House St. Barts." (This is not a real beach house, but it is a good example of how you can help someone plan their trip by offering free info. And if they haven't booked their place to stay yet, well, chances are they will click through to see the beach house.)

Reviews—The Good, the Bad, and the Ugly

Okay . . . so here is the reality part. Sure, we encourage you to put a beautiful vase of flowers on a table and then take the photo—but if you're not paying attention to your reviews, it doesn't matter how beautifully styled your property is. Reviews are where you will go up or down in the rankings. It's where potential guests see how you handle a bad review, solve a problem, answer a question, respond to a kind review . . . this is where they get to know the real you.

Make sure you have a good understanding of how reviews work on the booking platforms that host your property—each one has different rules. Some require reviews to be written within a short period of time, others allow you to delete a review but then you can't add another one. In addition, make sure you know other locations where folks can post reviews, and keep tabs on those sites as well.

How do you encourage your guests to write great reviews? Make it easy for your guests to write them. You should have a very good idea of what your guests will say in their review before it even goes up. In fact, you should know in advance what 90 percent of your reviews will be. And you should know this because of how you prepared your guests for your rental, how you communicated with them, and how you encouraged a 5-star review. Why does it matter to get a 5-star review? Because the better review, the higher you can get on your booking platforms when guests are searching by guest review rankings. And the higher you get on the site, the more likely it is for potential guests to see your property and book you! It doesn't get any more straightforward than that. With more and more short-term properties becoming available every day, you need to stay on top of this to make sure you don't get lost in the crowd.

You will get a bad review . . . no matter how amazing the experience may be. This happens to everyone. Don't take it personally, but do handle it as quickly and as professionally as possible. Your potential future guests read these reviews, and they will judge how you managed the situation.

Customer Service Success

Never . . . and we mean never . . . underestimate the value of great customer service, especially in the age of instant communication. In less than a blink of an eye, a customer can write a bad review that can turn away hundreds (maybe even thousands) of potential customers. This is our new reality. There are so many easy ways to make your customers happy and loyal, bringing friends and family along with them. With a good plan in place, you can handle anything from a great review to one that didn't go your way. From handling customer service to handling mistakes, we want to help you understand some of the issues you may come across in the boutique hospitality and vacation rental market.

First and foremost, love what you do or get out. There is nothing worse than saving all your money for an amazing vacation, heading out to your special place you booked, and being treated like dirt by someone who would obviously rather be somewhere else . . . anywhere else. Don't do this to your guests. Think long and hard about how your attitude affects your guests and reflects on your business. Be authentic, kind, and thoughtful . . . the end.

Whether you're doing "invisible service" (that is, you're not there yourself, but you provide lots of advice via websites, email, texts, and so forth) or if you provide full-on walk-throughs and breakfast foods, understanding your guests goes a long way in making them happy. Walking the walk, or the "customer's journey," is a great way to make sure the experience is the best it can be for your guests. There are times when the experience goes wrong, and being prepared for that is critical for the success of your rental business.

Let's take a walk in Jack and Jill's shoes. What do we mean by that? If every single step your guests take is a touch point, then you need to experience every moment of their journey . . . from finding you online, to reserving with you to getting to your location to parking to unlocking the door to walking in to where they set their stuff down to how they use your place (and the ease of it) to enjoying your location (park, beach, city, countryside) to checking out, and to staying in touch. You can do it yourself, or you can ask a friend to literally go through the process without any help from you. Where are the kinks? Did you forget a step, like where they park? Did you forget to leave extra pillows, sheets, and a blanket in the closet? Did you forget to leave instructions on how to use the TV? Did you forget to ask them to follow you on social media? Did you forget to follow up with a thank-you email and card? Taking this "customer's journey" will help you get a chance to work out all the kinks and to anticipate as many problems as possible.

To take your customer's journey, walk through the following steps:

Read Your Reviews: Without getting emotional, read the reviews. You need to hear what your guests are telling you.

Ask Someone You Know: Have someone walk through your property, your website, and listings, and take notes. They will see things that you have overlooked, just because you've looked at it for so long.

Own Up to Your Mistakes: They happen (so we hear). We have stayed at plenty of places where something didn't go quite right—where the fire alarm beeped all night because the battery was going dead, where the cat left us a present (a dead rat) by our front door, when we walked into our rooms only to find out that other people were already staying in them. . . . We could go on, but how the hosts handled the problem was what made us love them or be disappointed by them. Make sure your guests love you even more when you err than when you are perfect. That said, keep records of all your communications with your guests. Booking platforms make this easy to do. That way if you can't fix your mistakes, you can at least prove you tried (this may save your rear, and save you some big bucks, as well). So try to anticipate what a mistake might be. In a cold location it could be a burst pipe. In a warm location it could be a broken AC. Do you have people in place who can fix these things?

Walk the Talk: Some of our best travel stay experiences have not been the poshest places. Rather, they were in out-of-the-way locations, with the kindest, humblest folks who were happy to show us their home, their town, and their love of their neighborhood. Do your best to exemplify this ideal. Furthermore, make sure whoever works for you, especially if they are in contact with your guests, knows how important they are to your team. Remind them that they represent your property and your brand, and that they must truly care about the guests' experience. We truly believe people want to do a good job, but sometimes they need a little reminding about how the customer perceives them.

And, last but not least, be a good customer. You're always representing your business or company—at the bank, post office, the plane, a party . . . We live in a society where one of the first questions people get asked is "What do you do?" (Except our husbands, they get "Is that your beautiful wife?") You will increase your company's goodwill through your external activities, expressions of sincere kindness, and treating your employees with respect. At the end of the day, you want to enjoy your life, love what you do, and go to bed feeling good about who you are and the difference you made in someone's life.

Facts and Stories

If you have staff, or a welcome person, make sure they are the best they can be. The worst thing as a guest is to walk into a place and be met by someone who is on his or her phone, ignoring you or even looking bored or condescending (yes, this happens). Have a plan in place with your staff as to what they should (and shouldn't) say to guests. Their message should convey your brand, and above all, be welcoming. Whether it is your design, your décor, or your service, every first impression counts. It's worth noting that more and more locations are moving to invisible service—where the guests check themselves in and out, and never see any staff. There are times this works well, but you still need to make a great first impression. If you can't be there in person or if you choose to have invisible service, consider adding a lovely handwritten note that welcomes guests to your rental. The goal is to provide a personal touch even when you are not there in person.

Facts and Stories

According to *Forbes* magazine, one study revealed that a whopping 74 percent of people will choose companies or brands based on the experiences others shared online. It's clear that third-party endorsement is critical for today's socially engaged consumers.

Rosanne would have forgiven anyone anything at this moment when, returning from her run, she found breakfast on the patio ready for her. When in Rome . . . literally.

Once Upon a Time Before Airbnb by Rosanne

Venice, Italy: I had booked all our hotels for our two weeks in Italy months before, and the only night I was having trouble booking was the night of arrival in Venice. No problem, I figured. We will just find something when we arrive. Ha! Almost four hours later, and after visiting every hotel in Venice, we still had no place to sleep that night.

We stopped at a hotel that had no rooms available and were told for the millionth time there were no hotel rooms left in the city due to some special event. The porter, Arturo, in his broken English, said that if we wanted to we could stay at his apartment, because he sometimes rented out his extra room. (We later learned he was studying hospitality management at the local school.) This was to be my first such experience, with what many years later would turn out to be commonplace, thanks to services like Airbnb. I'm sure if he had offered me his sofa I would have said yes at this point. Sean (now my husband) agreed with him on the price, and then we were off.

It was very late as we headed to the neighborhood district in Venice. Arturo asked that we give him a few minutes while he set up the guest room. He said there was a nice pizza joint right around the corner if we were hungry, Pizza dei Voilgoil. I can still taste that slice of pizza. When we returned, Arturo took us to a room that was filled with books, a desk, and other items that had obviously been moved to the side of the room. It was definitely a home.

But what made me sigh in relief was that he had thoughtfully set up two twin folding beds on each side of the room. The beds had been made up with fresh sheets and blankets, and they were turned down nicely. He had placed a couple of towels at the end of each bed. After flying for hours, and after buses and boats and carrying my bag over who knows how many bridges, I felt so tired that I couldn't feel my feet. After all the day's trials and tribulations, looking at the turned-down twin cot you would have thought I had arrived at the Four Seasons. I almost cried and I slept so well.

The next day, we came back from our early morning run and he was up and ready with coffee. And I swear *everything* from his fridge was out on that table. He poured our coffee, and with a wave of presentation to the table he asked us to please help ourselves to anything we liked. I don't know where Arturo is today, but I have no doubt that young man who was studying hospitality management is having a lifetime of success.

Before

DESIGN THOUGHT PROCESS: SMALL TWEAKS FOR BIG RESULTS

This is Joanne's third vacation rental project with the same owner, who is all about improvements within a reasonable budget. This master bedroom area has been transformed. The old cabinet doors were removed from the closet spaces. They were reused to create a dramatic headboard for the master bed. Although it looks like the same wall, it isn't: An additional insulated wall was placed there to give some privacy (and dampen noise) from the new bathroom that replaced the extra-large closet. (Adding a master bathroom was important in this renovation, because this house had one full bathroom and 12 beds.) There is still a large closet in the bathroom area, and there is plenty of dresser and storage space in the room itself. A bold carpet, two wall sconces, bright white paint, some fun bedding, a custom throw pillow (made by Suzanne, an artisan who sells her handmade pillows on Etsy as Studio Tullia), and secondhand shop décor has given this room a new lease on life. The moment these rooms were done, Joanne started putting photos of them on social media, giving hints of the vacation rental that was opening soon. This was a great way to build excitement.

You don't have to wait to start your marketing, especially if you need to shut down for a while as you renovate. But you will need to plan ahead and get people excited and booking for advance dates. Put up a website with a drawing that says, "Coming soon!" Or run a promotion. The text might read, "Book now! Get a 20% off discount for the first 10 people who book!" There are numerous ways you can build excitement from your renovations. We suggest you visit Main + Mountain Bar & Motel's Instagram feed to see how they started getting folks excited about their renovation project.

After

Time Out, Don't Press Send

There are times when you host the guest from hell. Yes, you will get them—everyone gets them—so plan on it and you won't be surprised. Try to kill them with kindness. If that doesn't work, then ride it out if you can, document everything on your hosting platform, and put them on a never-to-rent-to-again list.

Make sure you stop yourself from sending emotionally charged emails or texts. Take a deep breath. Don't hit the send button. Rewrite the message. Can't do that because you are so mad? Then slowly back away from the computer or phone and do some deep breathing. Not enough? Then sleep on it. Remember, electronic communications never really go away. What you post on your booking platform is open to the public and is forever recorded—think of your future. If you are using a hosting platform to communicate, make sure your responses are professional and courteous—this is especially important for future references and protection. While you're at it, always put a positive spin on a bad or emotional situation. Good marketing is not only about what you do, it is also about what you don't do.

Saying Goodbye

Don't say goodbye forever. Many times, once the "sale" is made and the guest leaves the relationship ends. But it doesn't have to be that way. How do you keep good guests coming back again and again, or at the very least sharing their experience with friends and family? You do it by keeping them in the loop with beautiful lifestyle shots of your place, any specials or events you have going on, and what is happening near you. This helps former guests remember all the fun they had at your property. Keeping in touch starts with small gestures. After they stay with you, thank them for staying and ask them if there is anything you could do in the future to improve a guest's experience. Ask them if you can keep in touch with specials and other things. Hopefully you have asked them to follow your social media as well. Hey, you never know . . . it could be the start of a long and lovely friendship.

Before

DESIGN THOUGHT PROCESS:
CREATING CHARACTER

Would this kitchen make you want to stop scrolling through lakefront properties on a booking site? Not us. Joanne was asked to help transform a family vacation rental so that both the owners and rental guests could enjoy it. In the kitchen, the first order of business was to remove the upper cabinets, add wainscoting panels, and install reclaimed wood shelving. It made the kitchen feel bigger and brighter, and it gave everyone easier access to the plates, bowls, and mugs—items that also serve as the décor! It is not difficult to add reclaimed wood to a hood vent, and there are many step-by-step tutorials online for how to do this properly. Instead of tile, we used wainscoting paneling for the walls and backsplash. Affordable and unique lighting was added. The island is now a rustic table with a vintage butcher-block top. With all the special touches and pops of color, this new kitchen is a huge hit with the homeowners and their guests (who mention it in their reviews). Same kitchen, different rental results!

After

Chapter ④

More Info and Resources

This is not going to be your typical resource list, because we are not your typical gals. As mentioned throughout this book, we lean toward eco-friendly, reusing, and repurposing. We adhere to these principles because we truly understand that our choices make a difference. You can have it both ways—a great design and an eco-friendly plan—it just takes a little bit of research and some extra humph!

Using your favorite search engine, you can find everything you need within five minutes on the Internet. So we've decided to give you a few more important eco tidbits mixed in with a few resources we like to use. Our goal is to show you the things that work for us so that you can use them as guidelines to find out what works for you, your guests, and your property. Deal? Deal. Read it all (even if you don't need new flooring right now). You'll be surprised at what you learn.

Now that you've read the book (cover to cover, at least twice, and forgiven us for all the homework we gave you), you can decide what works best for you, your guests, and your property.

Joanne styled this bedroom owned by Wendy Lewis of Textile Trunk. Joanne wanted to show you how easy it is to change a space with some lovely textiles, a vintage table, chair, and lamp. It's an instant romantic French country feel—inviting and calming was our goal. Updating and changing a room can be as simple as adding décor details or as involved as blowing out walls and rearranging space.

Stuff for the Property

We all love going to our favorite home goods store and online sources for fixtures, appliances, furnishings, décor, and amenities. It is a fact. But we hope that you will consider reusing products that are already out there. Pay a visit to your favorite rebuild centers, secondhand shops, and architectural salvage stores. Go local, reuse, and rely on eco products first. Strive for other products to be a smaller percentage of your purchases. There are so many amazing products out there—all you have to do is take a little extra time and do some quick online searches. More and more, guests are looking for eco choices in their lodging experiences.

Furniture

There are thousands of options for furniture. Check out your local consignment shops and secondhand stores first. Once you've done that, then go online to sites like Craigslist, Chairish, and 1stdibs for some unique and fun finds. Then see who is making what in your state—you would be surprised how many local furniture and table makers there are. Quality over quantity will be their motto. Other furnishing groups we like are Ethnicraft, Shelby Williams, Cococo Home, and Lee Industries, just to name a few.

Utensils and More

Coffee maker, dishes, silverware . . . think consignment shops and secondhand stores. What do you still need to get? If you need to buy new, don't forget to print out your 20-percent-off coupon or your 50-percent-off-one-item coupons before you head out to your local kitchen and home goods stores.

Carpeting, Rugs, and Wood Floors

For carpeting and engineered wood, we like the company philosophy of Interface. Give them a try. If you are going for real hardwood, which is always our first choice when we can get it, go local or reclaimed—our favorite go-to for materials. Call your local lumber or salvage yard and ask if they have some leftover products or reclaimed materials—we always find some great deals this way. That said, the labor can be a little more if you go this route. Area rugs are very popular and a number of companies sell vintage and unique rugs. Chances are you can find a few in your area. Or go online—on Instagram alone, we can give you six stores we love: Old New House, Kennedy

Rose Interiors, Hamlet Interiors, Frances Loom, Flea Market Fab, and Kaya Kilims. If you see something you like, don't dither. Their rugs go fast.

Bedding

It's sad to say that cotton is one of the "dirtiest" crops in regard to eco-friendliness. (Rosanne, in the role of CEO for Pact Apparel, a fair-trade, eco-conscious organic cotton clothing company, saw this way too often and was proud to work with this company that really made a difference.) Fortunately, there are a ton of companies that are conscious about their cotton and linen products. You can easily use products from such companies for your guests' comfort and enjoyment. Here are a few bedding companies to check out: Rough Linen, Dunelm, Northern Feather, Parachute Home, and Boll & Branch.

For throw pillows, blankets, and throws we can recommend some fabulous artisan and fair-trade companies: Pendleton, VivaTerra, and Pine Cone Hill. Look through listings on Etsy for more. Have some fun with these, while supporting some really cool artisans. When using throw pillows, get those that have zippers or ties so you can wash them on a regular basis.

Toiletries and Cleaning Products

Your choices for toiletries and cleaning products are just as important as what you pick for furniture. Everyone in the industry is moving away from the tiny plastic shampoo, conditioner, and soap bottles. So don't be the one that everyone is pointing at—move to refillable dispensers with natural products. Be the cool host! Try some local products as well. Take a peek at the offerings on Pineapple Hospitality's website for a variety of great products.

Facts and Stories

Something has got to be done to stop the proliferation of plastic bottles. According to *Green Lodging News*, 69 billion bottles are created each year and 38 billion of them go into oceans and landfills. Up to 90 percent of the 69 billion are not recycled. A plastic bottle in the ocean will take 700 years to decompose. Plastic bottle recycling took a hit in early 2018 when China announced it would stop taking most of America's recyclables. Oftentimes, plastic bottles are burned in carbon-releasing, waste-to-energy plants. Please see Chapter 2 for some great options.

And let's not forget how important it is to have a clean place. Your guests and your housekeeping staff will love the fact you use products without harsh chemicals. Here are some of the companies that are easy to find and great to do business with: Seventh Generation, Mrs. Meyer's, Method, Better Life, Grove Collaborative, Branch Basics, and Ecos. And don't forget what we said about toilet paper, in particular, and paper products, in general—*recycled* is your watchword; 27,000 trees get cut down a day so we can wipe our butts (if we could, we would insert the blushing emoji here). Look for eco products when you purchase TP, paper towels, and napkins. Even the Trader Joe's brand of TP is recycled.

Photography and Video

Check out your booking platform for photography and video advice and links to service providers. Airbnb has great resources for photography: how to do it, how to improve your shots, and how to get ready for professional photographers. They also offer some great marketing tips. Airbnb's list includes some experts in the field of photography that are specific to the short-term rental market. Overlooked 2 Overbooked (www.overlooked2overbooked.com) is also a great resource for photography. They have e-newsletters, courses, podcasts, and services, and they will personally edit some of your photos.

As we have previously mentioned, to save money you can hire high school and college students to take photos and to shoot video. Find out what classes are offered in nearby schools, and then approach the teacher and ask if they have a student who would like a "real life" assignment. In our experience, the results have usually been great. We get some great video and photos, and at the same time we get to help students build their résumés. Of course, you get what you pay for, meaning that if the photos or video don't turn out like you had hoped, then you'll have to hire a professional. And don't forget styling. There are professional stylists out there. If you don't know any, your photographer will.

Creating more sleeping space can be as simple as adding a trundle bed. Joanne styled this room to look lived-in and inviting. Don't you just want to curl up in this bed and read a book for the afternoon? We do.

Podcasts You Should Listen To

We are both big podcast listeners. They get us through a 30-minute walk or a drive to a client's property. Okay, maybe we sneak in a little '80s rock as well. The problem is that most of the business, marketing, and design podcasts we listen to are so informative that we wish we could take notes. It's usually not a problem, because (thankfully) the show's notes are on their websites.

Here are some great podcasts to help you in your endeavors: *Holiday Let Success* with Elaine Watt (we listen to her for lots of great tips and because we love her accent); *The Goal Digger Podcast* with Jenna Kutcher (not only one of our favorite podcasts for marketing tips, but she has recently become a short-term rental owner and has lots of ideas on that subject as well); *Vacation Rental Success* with Heather Bayer; *Vacation Rental Formula* with Mercedes Brennan; *Hotel Design Podcast* and *No Vacancy* with Glenn Haussman (these last two, both hosted by Haussman, are usually for larger hotels, but you can get lots of tips). We could go on, but that's more than enough to start. You'll soon find your own favorites.

YouTube Channels You Should Follow

Video has become an important part of the hospitality market, and you will want to jump on this bandwagon if you aren't already on it. Here are a few of our favorite channels on YouTube that cover this subject: HomeAway TV, Get Paid for Your Pad, Airdna, Short Term Rental University (STRU), and Vacation Rental Managers Association. For fun, you can also view archived videos that Joanne Palmisano did for DIY Network.

Websites That Know Their Sh . . . Stuff

Most of the podcasts and YouTube channels we've mentioned also have blogs. Be sure to seek those out, too. In addition, the following sites are always updated with great information for property owners: getpaidforyourpad.com, homeaway.com, airbnb.com, vrmb.com, tripadvisor.com, flipkey.com, airdna .com, flippinwendy.design.com, learnbnb.com, and lodgingmagazine.com. Also be on the lookout for local blogs—they'll clue you in on issues and events that are happening in your area.

Get With Your Peeps

Folks in the boutique hospitality industry and short-term rental market often get together and learn from each other. You can join us. The more we work together, the better we all will do. Antonio Bortolotti founded the Vacation Rental World Summit (vacationrentalworldsummit.com), and each year thousands of folks get together for this event in very cool places and learn loads. There is also a new Vacation Rental Women's Summit (vacationrentalwomen.com). Check out your local tourism summits, online groups (including LinkedIn), and other gatherings (virtual and in person). Be a part of our community.

Must-Read Books

There are a ton of books out there about investing in vacation rentals and real estate. Here are a few that we feel are really helpful (besides ours, of course). Visit your library and check them out. Skim through the various titles and then go out and buy the ones you know you'll be reading again and again.

Get Paid for Your Pad by Jasper Ribbers and Huzefa Kapadia

Vacation Rental Success by Joel Rasmussen

Make Money on Airbnb by Sally Miller

Overbooked by Elizabeth Becker

Money Making Vacation Rentals by Beth Carson

Build a Rental Property Empire by Mark Ferguson

The Vacation Rental Goldmine by Chris DeBusk

How to Rent Vacation Properties by Owner by Christine Hrib-Karpinski

100 Tips for Hoteliers by Peter Venison

Start and Run a Bed & Breakfast by Louise and David Weston

Of course, we would be thrilled if you read all three of Joanne's salvage books: *Salvage Secrets*, *Salvage Secrets Design & Décor*, and *Styling with Salvage*.

Articles We Think You Should Read

We read a lot of articles online (Rosanne more than Joanne, but to be fair Joanne makes some really cool crafts). Here are just a handful of articles we thought were interesting enough to pass along to you. Not only are these specific articles interesting, but the sources are ones we recommend you pay closer attention to—you might like them enough to sign up for their e-newsletters or to read their blogs. Obviously, more articles are always coming out, so stay on top of it and read every week.

Pinterest
"2018 Travel Trends: How Your Brand Can Reach Travelers Deciding Where to Go Next"
business.pinterest.com/en/blog/2018-travel-trends-how-your-brand-can-reach-travelers-deciding-where-to-go-next

Fast Company
"How to Make a Killing on Airbnb: Two Airbnb Experts Offer Tips to Make Your Property Rain Money"
www.fastcompany.com/3043468/the-secrets-of-airbnb-superhosts

Villa Marketers
"12 Expert Vacation Rental Marketing Ideas. Your Keys to Unlock Direct Bookings (Video)"
www.villamarketers.com/vacation-rental-content-marketing-ideas-for-seo-success

Pillow
"6 Tips for Boosting Your Vacation Rental SEO"
blog.pillow.com/6-ways-to-revolutionize-your-vacation-rental-search-rankings

Evolve
"How to Use Social Media to Advertise Your Vacation Rental"
blog.evolvevacationrental.com/how-to-use-social-media-to-advertise-your-vacation-rental

Guest Hook
"Here Are the Best Airbnb Descriptions We've Found"
https://guesthook.com/best-airbnb-descriptions/

Natura Water
"Eco-Friendly Hotel Ideas You Need to Implement Now"
www.naturawater.com/buzz/eco-friendly-hotel-ideas-you-need-to-implement-now

TripSavvy
"The 10 Best Eco-Friendly Hotels of 2019"
www.tripsavvy.com/eco-friendly-hotels-4122316

Artone Manufacturing
"5 Tips for Making Hotel Furniture Design More Eco-Friendly"
blog.artonemfg.com/blog/hotel-furniture-design-sustainable

1 Chic Retreat
"How One Airbnb Owner Is Killing It on Instagram and What You Can Learn from Her"
1chicretreat.com/one-airbnb-owner-killing-instagram-can-learn/

Well+Good
"If You're Looking to Get in Bed with More Eco-Friendly Brands, Here Are 15 to Start"
wellandgood.com/good-home/eco-friendly-bedding

Trivago
"The Inexpensive Hotel Amenities That Luxury Guests Now Want Most"
businessblog.trivago.com/inexpensive-hotel-offerings-luxury-guests

NRDC
"Can We Talk About Toilet Paper?"
www.nrdc.org/experts/anthony-swift/can-we-talk-about-toilet-paper

Vacation Rental Formula
"The Vacation Rental Welcome Book"
www.vacationrentalformula.com/the-vacation-rental-welcome-book

AirDNA
"5 Tips on Acing Your Airbnb Guest Communications"
www.airdna.co/blog/5-tips-on-acing-your-airbnb-guest-communications

Apartment Therapy
"Shh! Here's the Insider's Secret to Finding Remodeling Materials for Cheap"
www.apartmenttherapy.com/habitat-for-humanity-restore-tips-28438109

Get Paid for Your Pad
"3 Essential Tips to Write Effective Airbnb Photo Captions"
getpaidforyourpad.com/blog/airbnb-photo-captions

Lodgify
"7 Vacation Rental Books to Help Grow Your Business"
www.lodgify.com/blog/vacation-rental-books

Before

DESIGN THOUGHT PROCESS: MAKE A BATHROOM MORE THAN A BATHROOM

The Mountain Modern Motel (formerly known as the Painted Buffalo Inn) in Jackson Hole, Wyoming is a great example of how to have some fun. The bathroom has a "tiny house" kitchen feel. Catering to adventurers, the motel services a clientele who not only take showers, but who pack a lunch for a hike or make coffee before heading off to ski. So the bathroom was designed in a fun and unique way that offers function as well as aesthetic. The fun details include a vintage-inspired double drain board sink and an industrial faucet. The same mirror that once hung in the bed area (painted black) now hangs on sliders. This allows guests to fully check out the topographical map of the area behind it. These are "interactive" elements of design. There is a "gear" storage area as well as a fun word search and some other inviting, creative, and useful details. This design by Truex Cullins (with Joanne) is functional, fun, and it fits its location—a triple win!

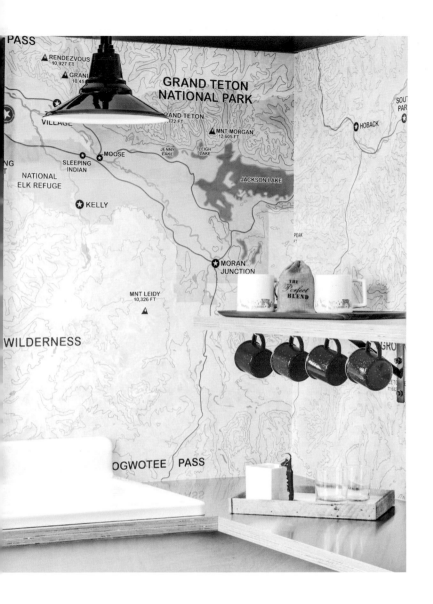

After

Guest bedrooms don't need a lot of stuff: calm and inviting, the best mattress and sheets ever . . . and clean. Those are the key elements for any good bedroom. This guest bedroom was part of an interior design project Joanne did for a private vacation home. The old window, which used to be among the windows in the barn, now serves as a beautiful mirror in the room. Not only does it help the small space look bigger and reflect natural light, but it brings the history of the building inside (same with the barn wood slider door). Simple, inviting, authentic, and comfortable. What more could you ask for?

Sources for Inspiration, Education, Trends, and More

Check out industry publications and subscribe to their e-newsletters. Here are a few of the ones we love:

Afar Travel (www.afar.com)

Airbnb Magazine (www.airbnb.com/magazine)

Apartment Therapy (www.apartmenttherapy.com)

Architectural Digest (www.architecturaldigest.com)

Boutique Design (www.boutiquedesign.com)

Design Hotels (www.designhotels.com)

Domino (www.domino.com)

Dwell (www.dwell.com)

Elle Décor (www.elledecor.com)

Eva Flores, Adventures in Cooking (www.adventuresincooking.com)

Green Lodging News (www.greenlodgingnews.com)

Here Magazine (www.heremagazine.com)

Hospitality Design (www.hospitalitydesign.com)

Jenna Kutcher (Goal Digger; jennakutcherblog.com)

Lonny (www.lonny.com)

Overlooked 2 Overbooked (e-newsletter; www.overlooked2overbooked.com)

Remodelista (www.remodelista.com)

Seth Godin (marketing blog; www.sethgodin.com)

Tablet Hotels (www.tablethotels.com/user)

The Venue Report (www.venuereport.com)

Travel and Leisure (www.travelandleisure.com)

TripAdvisor (e-newsletter; www.tripadvisor.com)

Trivago Business Blog (businessblog.trivago.com)

Before

DESIGN THOUGHT PROCESS: MAKE YOU FEEL LIKE YOU'RE ON THE WATER

In this cottage on the shores of Lake Champlain at Basin Harbor Resort and Boat Club, you could have been anywhere. Joanne redesigned the cottage to give it a nautical feel with some bold statement pieces like the vintage sailboat and wooden ship's steering wheel. She was thrilled when they peeked under the wall-to-wall carpet and found hardwood floors, which, of course, had to be refinished; they transform the space. Whenever possible, Joanne uses wool rugs in rooms because of their long-lasting quality, natural fiber, and because they are more eco-friendly than man-made rugs. By painting the paneling a bright white, the wood framed mirror and décor really stand out. The blue wall and stone countertop in the bar area liven up the space and give it a pop of color. The leather pull-out couch is a quality piece and the old coffee table was given a paint job. The end tables and lamps were found in storage on the property, so Joanne reused them to give the living room more lighting and useful surfaces. The custom linen ship's wheel shower curtain in the updated bathroom complement the nautical style. There were very few structural changes in the space, but it looks completely different.

After

We hope we helped you rock your rental . . . even a little bit!

Acknowledgments

Big Huge Thank You . . .

There are so many people in our lives we are grateful for, and we hope you all know who you are, but we will give a big thank-you shout-out again to remind you how awesome you are!

For this book, we couldn't have done it without the amazing team at Countryman Press: Róisín Cameron, Ann Treistman, Isabel McCarthy, Michael Tizzano, Nicholas Teodoro, and all the staff who made us look and sound great!

To our family, Mom and Dad, our sister, Julie, and our brother, Charlie, for all their support and keeping our egos in check with pithy one-liners. Joanne's daughter (and Rosie's niece) Gabrielle Booth, for taking some photos of us for the book and for not rolling her eyes (too much) during our giggle fits. And our husbands, Stephen Booth and Sean Roy, who have come to realize that when you marry one of us . . . you marry the other one, too.

And to all of you who helped us with this book, *grazie mille* (thanks a million). Jeannine Giordano, vacation rental homeowner; Julia Katrine, Julia Katrine Designs; Gideon Pollack, Forum Properties; Eliza Greene and Justin Hyjeck, Main + Mountain Bar & Motel; Becky Fair, vacation rental homeowner; Sean and Karen Lawson, Lawson's Finest Liquids; Julie and Brian Sullivan, Bear Mountain Inn; Bob Beach, Pennie Beach, and Brian Goodyear, Basin Harbor Resort and Boat Club; Jen Wyman, Accomplice Marketing; Kim Deetjen and all the folks at TruexCullins Architecture and Interior Design; Cari Cucksey and Vinent Iafano, Holly Vault Crossing House; Wendy Lewis, Textile Trunk; Heather Brown and Andrew Lynds, Mad River Barn; and all the amazing contractors, plumbers, electricians, artisans, and service folks who work with us on the numerous renovations and understand our crazy drawings, Italian hand signals, and speed-talking instructions to create amazing transformations that turn our frowns upside down.

Another big thank you to all the great photographers in the book: Susan Teare, Lindsay Selin, Molly Breton and Victoria Johnson of Molly and Victoria Co., Gabrielle Booth, Amanda Herzberger of Orchard Cove Photography, Alana Cushman, and Ryan Sheets. The folks at Mason Brothers Salvage, Five Corners Antiques, Barge Canal, Champlain Valley Antiques, and all the secondhand shops we frequent, for putting up with our craziness. And those who wanted to remain anonymous (you know who you are . . .), thank you.

References

Page 17: VRMB. "By 2020, Vacation Rentals Will Topple the Hotel Industry."
May 31, 2016.

Page 17: *Consumerist* magazine. "9 Things We Learned about How Few
Americans Are Regularly Taking Part in the Shared Economy." May 19, 2016.

Page 47: VRBO. "You Could Increase Bookings with Amazing Photos." 2019.

Page 49: *Lodging* magazine. "Eight Travel Predictions for 2019." October 19,
2018.

Page 60: *Realty Times.* "8 Paint Colors for a Standout Front Door?" September
28, 2017

Page 60: *Inc.* magazine. "You're Being Judged by these 4 Things." March 3,
2015

Page 110: *Hotel Management.* "Hotel Bedding Trends Promote Wellness,
Cleanliness." March 10, 2017.

Page 121: Natural Resource Defense Council. "Issue with Tissue: How
Americans Are Flushing Forests Down the Toilet." February 20, 2019.

Page 128: Vacation Rental Pros. "6 Tech Amenities Guest Need in Their
Vacation Rental." March 2017.

Page 138: *Hotel Business.* "Cleanliness and Comfort Top Everything Else in
Hotel Selection." September 11, 2017.

Page 150: Airbnb. "Photography that Pays for Itself." 2019.

Page 150: VRMB. "Good vs. Great Vacation Rental Photography." August 3,
2012.

Page 161: *The Atlantic* magazine. "Instagram's Wannabe-Stars Are Driving
Luxury Hotels Crazy." June 13, 2018.

Page 177: Pinterest Business Insight. "2018 Travel Trends How Your Brand
Can Reach Travelers Deciding Where To Go Next." August 24, 2018.

Page 184: *Forbes* magazine. "More than Awareness: Influencer Marketing's
Role in the Sales Funnel." May 29, 2018.

Page 193: *Green Lodging News.* "Creative Alternatives to Plastic Water Bottles
Emerging for Hospitality." April 4, 2019.

Photo Credits

All photos by Joanne and Rosanne Palmisano except those noted below:

Photography © Alana Cushman: Pages 28, 100

Photography © Gabrielle Booth: Pages 14, 27, 63, 70 (right), 136 (top), 140 (right), 154, 208

Photography © Lindsay Selin Photography: Pages 2, 18, 25, 37, 51, 59, 73, 74, 75, 81, 92 (right), 99, 102, 109, 113, 129, 131, 135, 137 (right), 141, 142, 157, 159, 171, 187, 195, 202

Photography © Molly and Victoria Co.: Pages 56 (top), 64, 77, 85, 86, 105, 123, 127, 136 (bottom), 153, 163

Photography © Ryan Sheets, Sheets Studios: Pages 33, 78, 90, 160, 200 (right), 201

Photography © Susan Teare: Pages 41, 42, 89, 101 (left), 115, 140 (left), 148, 158, 175, 190

Photography © Orchard Cove Photography: Pages 5 (bottom), 53, 57 (top), 95, 205

Index

Note: Page references in **bold** indicate text in photo captions.